SELF-PUBLISHING:

YOU

CAN DO

THIS!

What You Need to Know to Write, Publish & Market Your Book

Karen Hodges Miller

Open Door Publications

Self-Publishing: You Can Do This!
What You Need to Know
to Write, Publish & Market Your Book

Second Edition Copyright© 2022 by Karen Hodges Miller
First Edition Copyright© 2017 by Karen Hodges Miller

ISBN: 978-1-7328202-5-8

Published by
Open Door Publications
4182 Olde Judd Dr.
Willow Spring, NC 27592
OpenDoorPublications.com

Cover Design: Eric Labacz, labaczdesign.com

This book is dedicated to my great virtual writers' group, Wendy, Jan, Sherri, and Jack. Thanks for reading my book, and thanks for putting up with all my critiques of yours.

Contents

Introduction
to the Second Edition

You must reinvent yourself every five years.

These words of wisdom were given to me by a business coach I interviewed for a magazine article a number of years ago. It has proved to be a good rule to live by for those of us in the publishing business. It seems that every time we get a handle on the latest trends, the newest apps, the current best practices—everything in publishing changes. And in the past two years, it is even more important than ever to be aware of the changes in publishing.

The tried-and-true methods just aren't working anymore in many businesses. Luckily for authors, the "COVID years" have been good for many of us. Many more people are reading, and many more people are writing. There are new apps to help people write, improve their grammar, keep track of their plots, format their books, and, of course, market their books. And some of the "best practices" I wrote about in 2012, 2014, and even 2018 have changed or just no longer apply.

What hasn't changed is that the competition on Amazon and other bookselling sites is enormous and getting bigger all the time. More than two million books are published in America every year. Many of them are awful. Many of them are undiscovered gems just waiting to find readers. There is no longer room in the publishing world for boring covers, bad grammar, poorly edited and proofed writing, or any of the other myriad ways in which authors allow their books to scream "unprofessional" to readers.

How will you make your book stand out from the crowd? How will you let your potential readers know that yours is a book they must read?

There is no one right way to publish a book. If you read websites by self-publishing experts, you will find a lot of rules about what to do and what not to do. Some are valid. Some were valid last year but are no longer. Some I disagree with. Some I embrace.

While there is no one right way to publish a book, *there is one very wrong way to publish.* That is to upload your book to Amazon and expect it to become an instant best seller. Readers will not buy your book if you don't let them know it's there. The day you aren't marketing your book is the day your book is not selling.

No matter what stage of the process you are in, this book can help you. Read on to find out how to write, publish, and market your book today.

Part 1
Write

Being busy does not always mean real work. The object of all work is production or accomplishment and to either of these ends there must be forethought, system, planning, intelligence, and honest purpose, as well as perspiration. Seeming to do is not doing.

Thomas A. Edison

Chapter 1
Unlock Your Ideas

When I first began writing on the subject of "how to write a book" in 2009, it was with great reluctance. I'd been working as a writer for more than twenty years. I'd edited and coached authors for a number of years, helping them develop their own books. I was published weekly in various newspapers and magazines. I didn't think I needed to write a book for credibility. I thought my credentials as a journalist, freelance reporter, editor, and publisher spoke for themselves.

I was arrogant. I'll admit it. And I was a little afraid. What if I didn't really have enough to say to fill a book? I didn't understand I had a process for taking an idea and turning it into a book—a process that had worked for many authors and would work for others.

"I work with each author where I find them. Every person I work with is unique, and their books are unique. I customize what I do to each particular writer," I protested whenever it was suggested I write a book on my process of coaching writers.

Luckily for me my friends and business colleagues did not allow me to get away with this nonsense.

"Everyone has a process," my business coach told me. "You just need to think about how you work with people. What advice do you routinely give to them, what steps do you lead them through? Once you do that, you will see you really do have a process that you follow."

"Everyone needs to improve their credibility and their visibility. You are out there speaking about your work. You need a book," said a marketing expert.

Eventually—reluctantly—I listened. I'm so glad that I did.

My first book on writing was titled *Unlocking Your Ideas*. I then wrote *Finish Your Book* (with Lorette Pruden) and *Sell Your Book*. I was then asked by People Tested Books to write *What's the Deal With Self-Publishing?* By the time I had finished with that book, I found that *Unlocking Your Ideas* was outdated so I needed to go back and rewrite it. It became *Write Your Book*. In early 2021 I wrote *How to Sell Your Book Today*, which focuses on social media techniques for selling your book. And now more time has gone by so it's time for an updated second edition of this book. And as I've been writing it, I have realized that I need another book, which I will call *Authorpreneurs*—but more on that later.

There are a lot of great books out there on the subject of writing books; a few of my favorites are *How to Write a Damn Good Novel* and *How to Write a Damn Good Novel II* by James N. Frey and *On Writing* by Stephen King.

How is this book different? I do touch on how to write because you can't publish if you don't get that book finished. But this is a workbook for people who want to take the next step after writing their book. They want to publish. I want my readers to use this book. Scribble in it (or highlight if you've bought the e-book version).

Writing is a discovery process. If you follow the steps I detail in this book, you will develop an outline to help keep you on track as you write. No matter how carefully you stick to that outline, you will also discover new ideas and develop new theories along the way. Whether you are writing fiction or nonfiction, whether you are writing a memoir or a practical how-to book, you will learn new information and formulate fresh theories and concepts. ***Writing a book is about unlocking your ideas and allowing them to grow in the light of day.*** It's fine to add those new ideas that don't stick to your original outline—as long as they don't take you too far from where you want to go with the theme and the purpose of your book.

Writing is exciting, it is fun, and it is hard work. It also takes time, it takes patience, and it takes belief in yourself to move from writing just for yourself, to letting a few friends see your work, to putting it out there for the whole world to see.

Set Your Goals

How long have you been thinking about writing your book? You may have wanted to become a writer your entire life, or you may instead have recently come to the realization that you have something to say and that the best way for people to hear you is through a book. It really doesn't matter where or when you decided to write your book. You may have written a few pages or made some notes, or you may have spent a lot of time planning your book in your head without ever actually sitting down to write it. What matters is now that you have made the decision you won't allow your dream to gather dust in a desk drawer or a long-unopened computer file.

Writing a book is difficult. If you've never written anything longer than a three- or four-page report, or even a ten-page short story, taking on a project as large as a book probably seems like a daunting task.

I have been writing most of my life; I've written short articles as well as long, book-length projects. I began my career as a newspaper reporter and editor, yet only after several years of writing on a daily basis did I decide to strike out on my own as a freelance writer.

Throughout my years as a freelancer, other writer friends often asked me to edit books they were writing. After working with several writers, I noticed a pattern. Many started their project with great enthusiasm, writing every day, getting up at four a.m. to finish a chapter, or staying up long after midnight.

After a few weeks or months of this type of schedule, their fervor waned. Real life intervened; the kids got sick, the job required overtime, a vacation or illness in the family disrupted the regular routine. The excuses were many and varied, and because they were invented by writers, they were all very, very creative. But no matter how creative the excuse, in the end it was always the same story: The book never got written.

A few of the people I worked with did finish their projects and went on to publish their work. Even though I began to work as a book editor for more and more authors, I noticed the success rate for finishing projects never improved; it remained about one in five. Then one day I got a call from a person who worked as a career coach, teaching young people how to become more successful in advancing in their careers.

Bob had never written a book before, but he told me he planned to write one in three months and have it published before Christmas. It was May. I laughed.

I'd known many people with years of experience in writing who couldn't finish writing a book in that kind of time, let alone deal with all the other details of book publishing such as editing, proofreading, designing a cover, and getting the book printed. But Bob was enthusiastic and insistent, and he also planned to pay me, so I agreed to work with him.

It was a great experience for both of us. We learned from each other. I taught Bob about the art of writing, and as I read his work and talked with him, I learned about planning and project management, budgeting time, and goal setting. Bob met all his goals, completed his book, and published it by Christmas. Working with Bob was my first experience in the techniques that good coaches—whether they are coaching sports or business, about life or writing—use to help their protégés meet their goals. Since that time I've not only read and studied more on coaching, I've worked with other coaches who also wanted to write books. As I learned from each person I worked with, my success rate in helping my clients finish their book projects also began to increase.

Writing a book is hard work. I will remind you of that often throughout this book. Writing requires time, creative energy, a sense of purpose, and a plan. It is often this last step—a plan—that writers forget about. You would not hop in your car and start a road trip from Florida to California without making preparations such as researching places to stop along the way, arranging a tune-up for your car, and obtaining a roadmap or GPS to guide you. A book is no different. Before you begin to write, you must do the planning.

As a newspaper reporter I learned the Five Ws and H of Writing: Who, What, When, Where, Why, and How. These very basic questions not only work for reporters but are a great start for authors. Using them will help you decide what you will write and are also an important starting point to help you unlock and develop your ideas, plan and organize your work, and complete your book. If you follow the process outlined here, by the time you have finished reading Part 1 of this book you will be well on the way to having your own book finished. And that's the first step in self-publishing.

Chapter 2
The New Rules of Publishing

As I've already mentioned, publishing your book is not the first step in the process; it is just one step out of many. I've found over the years that clichés often have some truth in them. So "begin with the end in mind" (or at least the middle), and you will find it is easier to end up where you want to be. I have found when I speak with writers who have never published a book (as well as a few who have published several) that many of them are stuck with old ideas, outdated facts, and outright myths about the publishing industry, the process of publishing a book, and the best ways to reach readers. Here are a few of the old rules of publishing and some new rules to replace them.

1. **Old Rule:** Once you've written your book and found a publisher, the hard part is over.
   New Rule: Writing isn't easy, but for many writers, the really tough job is marketing because they have little or no experience with it.

   Today's author is a small business owner. You must learn everything you can about accounting, distribution, royalty payments and percentages, networking, marketing—all the details that the owner of any other business must learn. You must decide what you can do for yourself and when you need to hire experts to help you. The stereotype of the solitary writer slaving away in the garret is just that: a stereotype, and an outdated one at that. You need a team to publish a book.

2. **Old Rule:** There is only one type of publisher and one method

for publishing.

New Rule: There are multiple methods of publishing and hundreds of publishers to choose from so find the publisher that is right for you—or self-publish.

The traditional "big six" publishers (Hachette, Macmillan, Penguin Group, HarperCollins, Random House, and Simon & Schuster) became the "big five" a few years ago when Penguin and Random House merged, making it all the more difficult for new writers to break into publishing with one of these large publishers. (Reportedly, Penguin Random House has been working to buy Simon & Schuster for several years. If that deal goes through it would become the "big four.")

The current "big five" traditionally look for blockbuster books and famous authors. If you don't already have a name for yourself, a social network following, or other databases of several thousand or more people who are waiting for you to write that book so that they can purchase it, I suggest you skip the traditional publishers and find an alternate method. There are small, independent publishing houses, educational publishing houses, self-publishing companies, and publishers with various "hybrid" publishing plans. You can do the research and do as much of it yourself as possible. Look at all your options before you decide which is the best one for you.

3. **Old Rule:** First, you write a book proposal, then you find an agent who finds a publisher and negotiates a contract with an advance.

   New Rule: Unless you are set on traditional publishing, bypass the agent and do your own research to find the publisher and publishing model that is right for you.

   The big advance is a thing of the past unless you are already a very well-known author whose name guarantees sales. Save yourself time and frustration. Instead of searching for an agent, do your own research on the different publishing options available to you, and the companies that are involved with each. The more informed you are, the better the decision you can make regarding the best ways for you to publish and market your book.

4. **Old Rule:** It takes two years or more to get a book to market.
   New Rule: You can write and publish your book in a year or less. To really make a name for yourself as a writer you need several books. Plan to publish a minimum of one book a year for several years if you are writing nonfiction and two to four books per year if you are writing fiction.

   I don't want to minimize the need for the rewriting and editing process—it's very important to have an excellent professional editor look at your work, particularly if you are going to self-publish. However, much of the time lag between acceptance by a traditional publisher and finally seeing your work in print has to do with old ideas on marketing, printing, and distribution. These days you can easily publish a professional book in a matter of months—if you work with the right professionals who can help you through the process.

5. **Old Rule:** Your publisher will handle all the marketing for your book.
   New Rule: No matter who your publisher is, or how large a company, to make your book a success you must be prepared to do your own marketing.

   This "rule" has always been a myth. Best-selling authors take an active role in marketing their own work. They not only make appearances at book signings but also develop seminars, attend conferences, are active on social media, and find as many ways as possible to meet their readers. You are the best person to market your book. Who else has a bigger interest in making sure it is a success?

6. **Old Rule:** Bookstores are the best way to reach your readers.
   New Rule: Your readers can be found in many places. Partner with businesses that target your readers, use social media and e-book discovery websites to get your book to its target readers.

Less than half of all book sales are actually made in bookstores. Books are sold in a wide variety of retail stores, from large chain drugstores to tiny boutiques. They can be found in museums and gift shops and craft stores and sporting goods stores. They are sold on websites, at seminars and workshops, at conferences and trade shows. Where are your readers? They may not be at the bookstore. Think about where you need to go to find them.

7. **Old Rule:** An e-book isn't really a book. You aren't a "real" author unless you have a paper book.
   New Rule: E-books are here to stay, and you need one!

   It wasn't too many years ago that people were questioning whether e-readers and e-books would last. At the start of the pandemic in March 2020, e-book sales quickly increased eighteen percent over March 2019. Store closings and shipping delays obviously increased the demand for e-books. And once readers found out how convenient they were, they have stuck with them. E-book sales have continued to be about twenty-five percent higher than they were before the pandemic. Even as we have returned to shopping in stores, many people will continue to stick to e-books for the convenience. No matter what genre you are writing in or whether you are writing fiction or nonfiction, e-books should be an important part of your book marketing plan.

8. **Old Rule:** You don't need social media to market your book.
   New Rule: Social media is one of the best ways to let people know you are out there.

   It doesn't matter whether you love Twitter, Facebook, TikTok, and Instagram or you hate them. If you are an author with a book to sell, you need to be using social networking sites. Today, social media marketing is one of the best ways to spread the news about your book.

9. **Old Rule:** I can just put my book on Amazon, and people will

find it.
New Rule: If you aren't marketing, you aren't selling.

The new rules of publishing, printing, and marketing books mean there are hundreds of thousands more books available to readers each year. How will your readers find your book in such a crowded field? If you aren't telling people about your book, they won't go looking for it on their own. There is no "write it and they will come." You have to give your potential readers a roadmap to find your book.

10. **Old Rule:** I'll just sit at my desk and write.
New Rule: You need to be out there meeting people. Yes, many people are still reluctant to go to in-person events right now, but that's where social media comes in. You must interact with people to sell your book—whether through in-person book signings, seminars, or other networking, or through *actively* engaging with people through social media.

Remember those solitary writers in the garret I mentioned in Rule 1? Well, the only part of the stereotype that is true is that they are probably starving. Most writers I know are rather shy and don't really enjoy large crowds of people—and often don't want to open up about themselves on social media, either. If you want to sell your book—I mean, actually make some money on it—you must consider developing a seminar, attending a trade show, arranging book signings, meeting with book clubs. Most of these things can be done virtually these days. Just make sure you are getting yourself and your book in front of your readers.

Now that you have spent some time thinking about your endgame, let's go back to the beginning and discuss the first steps in writing your book.

Chapter 3
Why Write a Book?

Why do you want to be an author? Notice I said author, not writer. What's the difference? Writers may choose to never publish their work for others; they may leave it untouched in a desk drawer or on a computer file. There are many great reasons to write for yourself, and only yourself, but having the desire to publish your work for others to read—to influence, to teach, maybe even to preach—is the difference between being a writer and being an author.

About thirty or forty years ago educators and pundits declared the death of the written word. Television and movies had made reading obsolete, they said. Instead of reading a novel, people would wait for the movie. Instead of reading a newspaper, they would receive all their news from television.

Then the Internet arrived. Suddenly everyone needed—and wanted—to read again, and the arrival of a fast and easy way to publish our ideas meant that anyone with a website essentially became a publisher. However, the volume of information available these days, not only on the Internet but through books and magazines, means it is often difficult for a writer to get noticed. For readers, all this easily available information means wading through a seemingly endless number of poorly written blogs, boring articles, and irrelevant websites to find what is needed.

The best way to stand out in this vast ocean of information is to *make sure that your writing isn't just average, but is interesting, informative, and relevant to the reader.* Whether you plan to publish an article in a magazine or on a blog, develop a website for your business, or write a book, excellent writing is the best way to ensure that you get noticed for the right reasons.

There Are No New Ideas

With so much competition out there, you might ask yourself why you should finally go ahead and write that book you've always dreamed about. Other people have surely written something similar already. There really are very few new ideas in the world. Many people have told me they had a great idea for a book but gave it up when they discovered someone else had already written something similar. Don't let that discourage you.

It is barely two years since we first heard of COVID-19, and a quick check of amazon.com in late 2021 showed there were already seventy-five listings for books on the subject. They included everything from scholarly nonfiction to religious to political to children's books. There are even a couple of fiction books out there. One titled *Kissing the Coronavirus* has a cover of a woman kissing a green man. It is described as "steamy viral erotica," and has a ranking of 206 in the "humorous erotica" genre. Not bad for a first-time author one year after a book release.

If you are still not convinced that it's okay to write a book when there are already similar books published on the subject, take a stroll through your nearest bookstore (yes, there are a few of them still out there). You'll see entire sections of books devoted to the same topic. You don't need a totally new and unique idea. That's pretty difficult when you consider that archeologists have discovered "books" written on clay tablets from as early as 3000 BCE. Don't give up on your idea just because someone else has written something similar. You don't need a brand-new idea; you just need your own unique take on the subject.

In fact, I would suggest if you go to the bookstore or do an Internet search and find *no* books that are similar to your idea, then you should reconsider writing it. If no one else is writing about it, it may mean there are not enough people interested in your subject who want to read about it.

The Internet has redefined the niche market. It is now much easier to find that small group of people interested in a very narrow subject. Before cable television, for instance, there were only a few networks available, all aimed at large, mass audiences. Now not only are there channels devoted just to sports, but there is also a golf channel, a tennis channel, a college sports channel, and even a cricket channel and a horse racing channel. The Internet narrows niches even more. Instead of just blogging about football or basketball, for example, a blogger can write about only one team. Choosing the subject matter for your book is similar. Find your niche, then narrow and target it to a very specific market.

Why Write a Book?

In Chapter 1, I mentioned the Five Ws and H of journalism. Here is the first of those questions. This is the question you should ask yourself even before you sit down to begin to organize your book: *Why do you want to write a book?*

It is a question that many people, even authors who have written more than one book, have never asked themselves. There is no right or wrong answer to this question but knowing your answer will help you choose exactly what type of book you want to write—or choose between several ideas you have for different books.

Here are a few possible reasons for writing a book.

- *You always wanted to write a book.* You have had that idea in your head or that outline in your bottom drawer for years—or even decades. If you are a fiction writer, you have characters just waiting for you to breathe life into them. Now is the time to pull that manuscript out and get to work. If not now, when?

- *You know a better way.* You are a bookkeeper who is an expert in QuickBooks®; you are a business coach with a new method for business growth; you are a teacher with great ideas to share on education; you are a fiction writer with new worlds to explore. You have ideas, and you want to share them with the world.

- *You want to increase your credibility.* There is no better way to increase your credibility than by writing a book. In fact, one survey I read showed that people perceive a published author who does not have a PhD to have as much or more credibility as a person who does have a doctoral degree.

- *You would like to become the go-to pro.* With some marketing assistance, a book can make you the person that newspaper television commentators, radio hosts, or online bloggers call when they need to quote an expert in the field.

- ***You want to increase your business.*** I've heard many authors say they don't care if they ever sell a book. One put it this way: "Every time I give my book to a prospective client, it not only increases my chances of getting the job but also increases the amount of money I can ask for it."

So what's your reason for writing a book? Answering the following questions will help you clarify your objectives.

- What would you like your book to accomplish for you?
- How can your book help your business?
- How will your book help others?
- What other goals do you have for your book?

When the writing and publishing process becomes difficult, just check back to these pages. They'll help you remember why you are working so hard to complete your book.

Chapter 4
Before You Begin

You may be so enthusiastic about starting your book that you can't wait to put your fingers to the keyboard and begin to write your first chapter. Before you begin there are a few things you need to think about. Taking some time now to organize your work and your thoughts will not only make it easier to write but will greatly increase your chances of completing your book, and of writing a book that sells. In this chapter we are going to think about the second and third Ws on our list of questions: Who and What.

Who Is Your Reader?

If you've spent any time at all in business, you've heard the phrase, "find your target market." As a writer, your target market is your reader. When I ask the writers I work with who their target reader is, the most common answer I get is "everyone," or some variation of the word, such as "every parent" or "everyone in business" or "everyone who likes to cook" or "everyone who reads mysteries" or another answer equally as broad.

Some people try to narrow it down a bit: "my audience is women" (okay, you've narrowed it to half the population) or "my audience is women between the ages of thirty and sixty" (now we've got it to one quarter of the population). All these answers are still too expansive to define your true target reader.

Before you begin to write your book, ***come up with as detailed a description of your target reader as possible.*** The more you know about your readers, the better equipped you will be in writing a book they will be interested in buying and reading.

Is your audience experts on your subject, or are they beginners in the field? Knowing the answer will help you adjust your vocabulary to the correct level. A book written for beginners that does not explain complex vocabulary specific to your subject will quickly turn off readers who are unfamiliar but want to learn.

Don't think this question is only for writers of nonfiction. Fiction writers must also think about the age and vocabulary of their readers. A "read-to-me" book, or one written for four- and five-year-olds who do not yet read, should have a higher vocabulary than a first reader. Why? Because young children's listening vocabulary and comprehension are greater than the words they can actually read for themselves.

Science fiction and fantasy are two other fiction genres that often require the writer to explain a new or different technology or world to the reader. If your characters live in a world different from our own, you must explain the rules of the world to the reader, including both the physics and the legal rules.

A second question to ask about your readers is their generation. Are they teenagers or over age fifty? Different age groups have their own slang and jargon or catchphrases, their own touchstones and icons. If your audience is around age thirty-five, referencing Frank Sinatra or Kennedy's assassination won't stir them; better to talk about Justin Bieber and 9/11 instead. If they are under twenty-five years old, Timberlake is passé; Megan Thee Stallion is one of the most popular singers right now. And, of course, COVID-19 will become the touchstone for Generation Z, the group who are in their late teens and early twenties right now.

I'm sure you are starting to understand what I'm talking about by now. Knowing who your reader is has a huge impact on how you write your book. Here are a few questions to ask yourself about your target readers.

- What is their gender?
- What is their age?
- What is their income level?
- What are their hobbies?
- What other books do they read?
- How much do they know about the subject of my book (i.e., is this written as a book for beginners or for experts)?

I often suggest writers think of a specific person who would enjoy reading their books. As you write, keep this person in mind. How would this person react to what you have written? Would the person understand the explanation or description you just wrote or be bored and find it too elementary? Would your reader chuckle or gasp in horror at the right places?

Write a description of your target reader. This person can be someone you know, or it can be a fictionalized, composite character. Either way, make your description as detailed as you can. When you work on your book, picture this person sitting at the table across from you. Write as if you are having a conversation with them.

Your Subject and Your Theme

How does the subject of your book differ from the theme of your book? *The subject is the topic of your book*—fly fishing in the Great Lakes, for example, or how to sell more widgets. *Your theme is the message you want your readers to remember.* It is your purpose, the reason you are writing your book.

Remember those high school English classes when you had to write compositions on the theme of exciting books such as *Billy Budd* or *The Crucible*? No one could have hated writing those essays as much as I did. Maybe that's why it took me years to admit that all writing—no matter how short or how long—must have a theme or purpose. If you don't have a purpose, why write at all? Once I learned this lesson, I became a better writer.

Remember, *your theme is different than the subject of your work.* Your *subject* is the topic that you are writing about. Your *theme* is why you are writing about it. To find your theme ask yourself these questions.

- What knowledge would I like my readers to gain from reading my book?
- What do I want them to think or feel?
- What actions would I like them to take after reading my book?

There are many reasons for writing a book. You may want to persuade your readers toward your opinion, introduce a new idea, or help them gain knowledge of a product or process. A few examples will explain it best.

- The theme of a book on salesmanship might be: "It is easy to increase your sales closing ratio by using these ten steps."
- A book designed to introduce beginners to economic theory could be: "Making sense of supply and demand is important for an understanding of both global and local economics."
- A life coach might have this theme: "Whether large or small, each of the choices we make has an impact on our lives."
- A theme for a fiction book aimed at middle school readers might be: "All actions have consequences."
- A theme for an adult fiction book could be: "With compassion comes forgiveness."

Write Your Theme

Notice each of the themes I cited as examples were only one sentence long. How long was your theme?

The first time you write your theme it may be a paragraph or two. That's an excellent place to start, but if it has taken you that many words to describe your theme, you are either unclear about your purpose, or you are attempting to include too many themes or purposes for your book.

Take a look at your paragraph and try to condense it. If you are having trouble, ask a friend to help you. Rewrite it, cutting out any ideas that are not essential. Don't stop until you can state your theme in one to two sentences. Then write your theme in a notebook, on your computer—anywhere where you can easily refer back to it. Keeping your theme in mind will help you keep your book on track.

Chapter 5
Organize Your Book

Finding your theme is probably the hardest part of writing a book. Now that you have discovered it, I know that you want to get started on writing your first chapter. However, there is still some organizational work to do. Your next step is to create an outline. Don't panic! I don't mean those formal outlines you were taught back in high school English class with Roman numerals and capital letters, although I must admit that's the type of outline I prefer. You can make your outline in any way that feels comfortable to you. You aren't getting graded on this outline, and no one else, except possibly your editor or writing coach, needs to see it.

I know several writers who use a "mind map" (a graphic way to diagram your book). Other writers' "outlines" are made on Post-it® Notes or index cards with one topic or idea written on each. The cards are then laid out on a large surface and arranged and rearranged until the order feels right. Another author took this idea to the next level. She painted her walls with dry erase paint, which turns a wall into a giant whiteboard. She can now scribble her ideas all over the walls of her room.

It doesn't matter what method you use to organize your book, but you do need to *decide how many chapters you will have and what basic information will go in each chapter.*

In addition to your overall theme, each chapter should also have its own mini-theme or purpose that works to enhance and move the reader forward in understanding the overall thesis of your book. If you are writing nonfiction, now is the time to think about what material you want to include in your book and in what order it should be presented. For example, if you are writing a book on digital photography, the purpose of your first chapter might be to introduce the reader to some of the differences between camera phones and digital cameras. The purpose of another chapter later on could be to discuss different exposure options.

If you are writing fiction, develop the basic plot of your book and the characters. Write a few sentences or a paragraph about what will happen in each portion of the book. Many fiction writers also find it helpful to write a short description of each of their characters.

Don't worry if, while you are writing, your characters themselves inspire new ideas that weren't in your original outline. Don't let that outline constrain your writing. *If your characters are whispering to you that they need to do something else, follow them, at least for a little while.* You can always rein them in if they go too far afield. As one writer jokingly pointed out to me, "There is always the backspace key!"

Your outline is an organizational and memory aid only. Spend only enough time on it so that in a couple of weeks or months when you are ready to write Chapter 6 you don't need to spend a lot of time figuring out exactly what you had planned to write about. Taking some time now to outline your book will make writing it go faster later on. Don't spend a lot of time perfecting the grammar and style of your outline. One writer may need only a few words or phrases to remember what is planned for each chapter. Another may need to write full sentences or paragraphs.

I suggest you include your title, theme, and a short summary for each of your chapters, your introduction, and conclusion in your outline. Once you have done that, you are ready to start writing your book.

Chapter 6
Pronouns and Other Controversial Issues

Mid-century modern may be fashionable when it comes to your décor, but the grammar rules you were taught in the mid-twentieth century and even later need to be sent to the recycling center unless you want to appear dated or, even worse, offend your readers.

In the early part of the twentieth century, gender inclusiveness in writing meant straining the language to come up with female versions of titles or careers that had long been seen as masculine. "Aviatrix" is one such word. And is someone a "chairman," a "chairwoman," a "chairperson," or just a "chair?" The title "Ms." sounded odd when it was first used in the early 1980s, and there was a time when, in a second reference, a man was always referred to without the use of the title "Mr.," while women always had a "Miss" or "Mrs." in front of their name in second references.

Back in the day we were taught that "he" was the universal pronoun that stood for both "he" and "she." In the 1970s we began striving for "gender parity" or "gender inclusiveness" in much of our writing. That used to mean alternating paragraphs, sometimes using "he" and sometimes "she" or, better still, using the awkward sounding "he or she" or the even more awkward s/he. Others tried to rewrite sentences so that the plural pronoun "they" could be used in a grammatically correct way.

Language is fluid. It is changing all the time. New words come into fashion; old words take on new meanings. As a writer, part of your job is to stay up-to-date. This is not a political discussion; it is not a discussion a whether you are "woke" (a fine example of an old word that has taken on a new meaning) or not. It is a discussion of how these ideas affect our writing every day, no matter who our audience or our topic is.

Using Gender References in Nonfiction

The way in which you use pronouns is most important if you are writing nonfiction. Here are a few clear-cut rules for "gender-neutral" writing.

1. Don't constantly assign the same gender pronoun to certain jobs. Nurses are not always female. Police are not always men.

2. Make sure your sentences don't encourage bias. For example, this sentence—"The female doctor walked into the room."—assumes that most doctors are male. Just use the word "doctor," then in the second reference use the correct pronoun for the specific person you are referencing.

3. Be careful about titles that indicate a person's marital status. Use only the last name in a second reference, no matter the person's gender or title.

4. Do not refer to a woman by her first name only if you would refer to a man by his last name or with a title. This connotes disrespect. We would not refer to President Biden as "Joe," and that's not the way we referred to him when he was the vice president, yet I have heard the current vice president referred to as "Kamala."

5. H/She is stylistically awkward. Only use it in form letters, contracts, or other similar writing. Avoid it in a nonfiction article, book, or other piece of writing.

6. "He or she" is slightly less awkward if used only occasionally. It can start to feel strained if used too often. Some people may object to always using "he" first in the phrase; however, switching to the less common "she or he" can feel disruptive to the flow of a sentence.

Some good replacements for "man"

• **One:** Star Trek writers later changed the famous phrase "where no man has gone before" to "where no one has gone before."

• **Folks:** The song "God Rest Ye Merry Gentlemen" is now

often sung as "God Rest Ye Merry Gentle Folks."
- **The common man:** the average person
- **Mankind:** people
- **Mailman:** postal worker
- **Congressman:** legislator
- **May the best man win:** May the best person win

Nonbinary Gender References

The problem is that the English language has no good gender-neutral word to substitute for "he" or "she." Most of our discussion so far assumes that the person we are referring to considers themselves one of these two genders. Until recently there were no singular, gender-neutral pronouns. In recent years people have come up with some alternatives. These include:
- **Zie**
- **Sie**
- **Ey**
- **Em**
- **Ve**
- **Ver**
- **Tey**
- **Ter**

These are just a few of the pronouns, and do not include their conjugations. For more information on this subject, check out https://uwm.edu/lgbtrc/support/gender-pronouns/.

When writing about a person, particularly in an interview article, *always* use that person's preferred pronoun. It does not matter whether or not you feel it is silly; it is the polite and respectful thing to do.

So what can you do when you're faced with one of those gender-neutral or gender-ambiguous language situations? The best option may be "they," even though it hurts my grammar-loving heart to suggest it.

Also consider the type of publication for which you are writing. A professional or academic journal will have different standards than a trade magazine. Always check with the publishers before you make assumptions and offend someone unnecessarily.

"They" Is the New He or She

"They" is becoming accepted in spoken language, even when we are referring to one person. You are probably already using it, particularly if you don't know the identity of the person you are discussing. For example, you might say, "I saw them go into the store," when you don't specifically know the person you are talking about.

To many ears it will sound best if you can make your sentence plural, but that is not always possible. Using "they" as a singular pronoun will offend some strict grammarians but, again, it is becoming more common in all but the most formal written language. The *Oxford English Dictionary* even traces the use of the singular "they" back to the fourteenth century.[1] I'm going to make sure I tell my English teacher friends and family about that one! *Merriam-Webster Dictionary*,[2] *The Chicago Manual of Style*,[3] the *Associated Press Stylebook*,[4] and the Grammar Girl website[5] also list it as acceptable.

Of course, offending people or not offending people is really what this chapter is all about. The sad truth is someone is always ready and willing to be offended. The questions you should ask yourself as a writer, are: Who do you care most about offending? When do you play it safe? When do take a chance on offending someone?

Fiction Issues

The issue in fiction is not usually gender. As the creator of the

---

[1] https://public.oed.com/search/singular+they/?post_type=post

[2] https://www.merriam-webster.com/words-at-play/nonbinary-they-is-in-the-dictionary

[3] https://www.chicagomanualofstyle.org/qanda/data/faq/topics/Pronouns/faq0031.html

[4] "Making a case for a singular 'they'": URL: https://www.apstylebook.com/blog_posts/7

[5] https://www.quickanddirtytips.com/education/grammar/gender-neutral-pronouns-singular-they

characters, presumably you know the gender of each and which pronouns they prefer. The issue in fiction is often: Will our characters do or say something that will offend the reader? And if so, is it worth it?

Let me state that I am not advocating any particular political, social, or other point of view. I'm asking you, as a writer, to be aware of what you are writing and how others may view it.

Here's an example from an author whose book I was recently editing. The book was set in the 1990s. One of the main characters, a male, teasingly says to another male character, "That's so gay."

It's a phrase that sounds "right" in the mouth of this particular character, who is not particularly politically correct even for the 1990s. But for an author writing in the 2020s, the question becomes: Is it so necessary to the story that taking a chance that it will offend the reader is worth it?

There is no one right or wrong answer to this question. In this case the author decided to remove the phrase because the book's audience is young and liberal and is likely to be offended by the phrase. Also, the phrase was not necessary to establish the personality of the character. *The phrase was not pivotal to the story so using it was an unnecessary risk.*

In some of the writing groups I work with we have discussed everything from the acceptability of a character giving milk to a cat to whether or not an author can write about characters of another race.

When deciding which pronoun to use or if to include something that might possibly be offensive, try to think like your readers. How will they respond to what you just wrote? When looking for beta readers, try to find people of different ages, genders, and ethnicity to look at your work. In the end you must decide for yourself if "risky" behavior, words, or phrases said by one of your characters is worth it or not.

Chapter 7
Write Your Book

Now we finally come to the exciting part! At last, it is time to sit down at your computer and start writing your book. There are hundreds of excellent books and websites already written and easily available to help you with the craft of writing. Several are mentioned in the Resources section of this book. Because so many resources are already available to discuss the craft and technique of writing, this book instead concentrates on just two of the many elements of writing that the authors who reach out to me struggle with the most.

The first is finding the time and the place to sit down at your computer and express your ideas. These are the **when** and **where** of writing your book. I include both time and place in discussing this element because both are so important to the second element I want to talk about: creative energy. This is the **how** of writing, which is a little more difficult to explain.

For a writer, creative energy is that unique combination of inspiration and motivation that gives a person the desire to sit down and write furiously because the ideas are flowing faster than the fingers can type. I call it "putting the *you* into your book."

Make It Personal

What do I mean by the phrase "putting the *you* into your book?" Whether you are writing fiction or nonfiction, a little bit of yourself must go into what you write. If it doesn't, your writing will be boring. Let's look at fiction first.

There is an old author's saying, "write what you know." In other words, if you don't have an understanding of the characters, of the time, and of the setting of your book, it will feel flat, and the characters won't seem real to your readers.

This does not mean you can only write about places you have actually seen or people who you have actually met. If it did there would be no fantasy or science fiction books. Think how much more boring our lives would be without classics such as L. Frank Baum's *The Wizard of Oz,* Jules Verne's *Twenty Thousand Leagues Under the Sea*, Frank Herbert's *Dune,* or J.K. Rowling's *Harry Potter* series.

Even if your book is set in a place of fantasy, the characters must feel real. They must speak and act like people your readers can identify with; their problems must seem real to your readers. To do that your readers must identify with the characters; they must have universality in their emotions, their desires, and their goals. In other words, they must think and act and have emotional reactions that feel real, that we, the readers, can identify with.

Consider the classic tale of King Arthur and Guinevere, which has been written about hundreds of times over the centuries. While we may love the thought of the power of being a king or queen or the adventure of being a knight going on a quest, that is not what has made this story last. What we identify with are the questions of honor, loyalty, and fidelity—questions all of us may wrestle with in our own way.

Don't Tell Me—Show Me

Making your story real also applies to the nonfiction writer. When you are writing a book on a nonfiction topic, it will be more readable if you open up and share with your reader. Put a little bit of yourself in your work. A book is not a business memo, even if you are writing on a business subject. A dry writing style makes for dry reading. Professional should not equal boring.

So how do you do this? Once again, put a little of yourself in your writing. Tell the reader a story. By this I mean two things: First, stories and illustrations add life to your work. Second, they often make it easier to understand complex ideas. So give real-life examples of situations and problems you have encountered and how you have solved them.

In addition to telling the reader about yourself, the overall tone of your writing should show who you are. Put a little piece of yourself into everything you write to give your readers a glimpse of the real person behind the pages. Here are two samples to show you what I mean.

The computer broke, and when I went to the Apple store, I was told that it would cost over $400 to fix it. I didn't have the money and wondered what I should do.

"Damn," I shouted as I pushed the "on" button on the computer and saw only the blue screen of death. This was the absolute worst day for this to happen. I had a deadline to make; Forbes Magazine *was paying me big bucks for an article, but I had to get it in today. It was the first time I'd been asked to write for* Forbes*; in fact, it was the first time I'd been asked to write for any national magazine. I had to get the story turned in by four p.m., and it was already almost noon.*
I packed up my computer and headed to the Apple store.

Which sample is more interesting? Which article would you rather read? In the first one, you really don't care what is going to happen to the person because there is no personality in the writing. It's the facts and just the facts.

The second sample adds emotion, conflict, and a hint of drama. What will happen to the writer? Will they get their computer fixed before the deadline? Adding personality to your work makes it much more readable. All these personal touches add up to you writing a book that is more attractive, and more sellable to readers.

Finding the Time to Write

For almost every writer finding the time to write is often the most difficult part of the process. There is no one way to write and no way to predict how long each book will take to complete. I am often asked how long it will take to write a book. That depends on many things—how long the book will be, how quickly you write, and how much time you can devote to the process. Writing is hard work. It takes time and discipline to sit down and work at your computer for a few hours daily or weekly, to clear your mind of the details of your day, and to focus on the book you are writing.

Working With a Coach or Editor

One of the best ways to complete a book in a timely manner and develop a work with the best chance of appealing to your target reader is to work with a writing coach or editor. What are the differences between a coach and an editor?

An editor will read and comment on your manuscript after it has been written and work with you to improve the grammar, content, and continuity of your work. A coach will read and comment on your manuscript but also assist you in organizing your material, set goals and timelines, and help you overcome any blocks or difficulties that may come up during the writing process. A writing coach can work with you even before you have written a single word.

The type of person you choose to assist you in writing your book, and when you decide to bring them into your project, is up to you, but I believe it is important to have an objective, knowledgeable person reading your work as you write. Often people ask a friend or relative to act as their editor, and this can be beneficial. Unless the person you have asked to edit your work is a professional in the publishing industry, there are areas in which they cannot help you, such as discussing the marketability of your work and being totally honest with you about the good and bad points in your writing. How objective about your work will your best friend or your mother really be? Sometimes it takes an unbiased person to give you a truly unbiased opinion.

Don't think I am suggesting that only beginning writers need an editor or coach. *Every professional writer has an editor.* When I worked as a reporter and as a freelance writer, I always worked with an editor, and over the years I have had the opportunity to work with editors I have loved and those I haven't. These experiences have given me strong opinions on what makes a good or bad editor.

What should you look for in an editor or coach? Obviously, the person should be someone with whom you are comfortable working. They should also be objective about your work. Writing is very personal. No matter what you are writing about or how much outside research or assistance or how many opinions you receive, in the end it is the product of your brain and your imagination. It is your baby. Sending it to an editor is like sending your child off to school for the first time. You are anxious. You want it to be liked. But you also want to see it improve. *A good editor will be objective about your work and ask the probing questions that push you to delve deeper and bring more to your writing*—often more than you ever knew was there.

It can be difficult, however, not to take the criticism personally. Editors can be tough at times, and a sensitive person who is not used to working with an editor can easily begin to feel as if they should never pick up a pen again. This isn't true. Your editor is trying to help you, not crush you. If you begin to feel this way, discuss it with your editor and find out what the person really thinks of your work. Once you have you can decide whether to continue to work with that person with a new understanding of their style and technique or to look for a new editor.

Editing and Rewriting

The only place you are expected to write something perfectly the first time—with no grammar or punctuation mistakes, no spelling errors, and every sentence marching in perfect order from thesis to conclusion—is a school exam. Your editor is not your teacher. You are not getting a grade. Your editor does not expect you to get everything right the first time—if you did you wouldn't need an editor. Why do I say this? Because I know so many writers who are afraid to show their work to a professional, experienced editor for fear the editor will find a mistake.

Of course they will! That is their job. Yes, your editor would like "clean" copy, in other words, copy that is reasonably free of basic grammar and punctuation mistakes. If there are too many grammar and spelling errors, it will take more time to go through the work, first checking for basic errors, then looking at the overall work for continuity, flow and interest. Plan to rewrite—probably more than once. Yes, you will want to give your best work to your editor, but it doesn't have to be perfect.

Editing is different than proofreading. Proofreading is reading a final draft for spelling and punctuation errors as well as for continuity in the size and type of font and other details. Editing is working with the content of the book to look at elements such as the thorough development of a thought or theme, the clarity of ideas and explanations, and making sure there are no inconsistencies.

I've seen editing parsed into various categories such as line editing, substantive editing, fact-checking, or copy editing. When hiring an editor you must definitely check with that person to make sure you know what is included in their definition of editing and how much will be charged. No matter what the editor calls it, if you really want to produce a professional, well-written book without plot holes, fact errors, word repetition, or grammar mistakes that grate on the ear of the average reader, you need an editor who will carefully look for all the things I mentioned above in your manuscript.

Finding Creative Energy

Have you ever woken up at three a.m. with a brilliant idea, hopped out of bed, and spent the rest of the night writing? Or grabbed napkins at a restaurant to capture the perfect phrase? Those are the times when writing is easy. Most of the time it is not, and if you wait for the right combination of time and inspiration to strike, it will take you years to complete your book.

Let me say it one more time: Writing is hard work. It takes time, and it takes creative energy.

What do I mean by creative energy? I mean that you need to feel refreshed, relaxed, and energized to write effectively. Most people cannot come home after working a difficult nine-to-five job, make dinner, help the kids with the homework, handle a few household chores, and still have the energy at eleven p.m. or midnight to sit down and write good work. Yes, I have known a few of people who can do this, but they are a rare breed.

Creative energy is that unique combination of inspiration and motivation that gives a person the desire to sit down and create—to write as fast as the fingers can type because the ideas are flowing. It can be difficult to tap into this energy if you are not regularly exercising your creative muscles—not just by writing but by living life in a creative way.

That's not as hard as it sounds. Take a few minutes every day to get out of your routine and do something to relax your mind and body, soothe your soul, and express your creativity. Take a walk, read a book for fun rather than just for information, change your driving routine so you see something new and different. Make time to talk with friends and time to be alone. Creativity comes from inside of you. If you don't take time to listen to yourself, you will never be able to hear your own creative voice.

You may be feeling frustrated about now because not only am I suggesting you find additional time in your schedule to write, but I also want you to find time to relax and nurture your creativity. It sounds as if I'm asking you to do the impossible. I'm not. Making time in your day to recharge your creative energy is the easiest way to finish your book in a timely fashion. How you do that is as individual and unique as you are. For some it will be a good run, for others a relaxing cup of tea.

Make a commitment to spend a certain amount of time each week working on your book. Just like going to a gym to exercise weekly, *exercising your writing muscles will keep them in shape.* And just like developing an exercise program, you need to schedule specific times to write. If you tell yourself, "I will write ten hours a week," without looking at your calendar and blocking out the time, it won't happen. The first thing you need to do is set up a writing schedule. Ask yourself these questions.

- **Approximately how many pages will my book be?**
  Obviously, a book that is 100 pages long will take less time to write than one that is 300 pages long.

- **When would I like to complete my book?**
  Now that you know how long your book will be, think about how quickly you write. If you can write three pages an hour, a 100-page book will take about thirty-three hours to write. If you can devote ten hours a week to your book, you can have a first draft written in three and a half weeks! Be practical here, and add in time for those unexpected things that always pop up and slow you down. Remember I said your *first draft* could be done in three and a half weeks. Don't forget to add in time for editing and rewriting. You might think editing will take less time than writing the first draft, and it might. Editing is when you polish the rough spots. I've known writers who spend a month or more

rewriting one chapter until they get it right. But if the chapter seems flawed, it is worth it. Taking that time is what makes a book great.

- **How many hours can I write each week?**
  Be realistic. If you set a goal of twenty hours, but already have a forty-hour-a-week job, spend an hour a day commuting, coach your son's hockey team two evenings a week, plus have all the usual stuff of daily living to attend to, you will not only fail to write twenty hours a week but will begin to feel guilty, and pretty soon you won't be writing at all. I recommend somewhere between six and ten hours, but if you can only find two hours a week, don't despair—use them.

- **When can I write?**
  The good news is you don't need to schedule a five- or ten-hour block of time; you will probably be less productive if you do that. Schedule between three and five separate blocks a week. That way if an emergency occurs and you miss one session, you still have other times blocked into your schedule to work on your book. Choosing too short a time period to write can be just as much of a problem as choosing too long a time period. One aspiring writer I know mentioned he was having trouble concentrating on his work. As I questioned him about his problem, I learned he scheduled fifteen minutes of writing time daily. While he was faithfully sitting down to write each day, he was accomplishing very little. By the time he got settled, looked over the work he had done the day before, and picked up the thread of his writing, his allotted time was over. I recommended he instead try writing three times a week for an hour or two at a time. He found he became much more productive.

- **Where can I write?**
  Sitting in the family room with the television on and your children squabbling is no way to work on a project requiring concentration. Before you begin your work, find a place where you are comfortable and won't be disturbed by the other members of your family.

Chapter 8
Writer's Block

Writers love to procrastinate so much we have even come up with our own special disease: Writer's Block. You've never heard of Carpenter's Block or Accountant's Block or even Dancer's Block, have you? It's not that writers are more prone to the problem; it's that we are more creative in coming up with excuses for why we don't finish that wonderful book we've always said we would write. The best news about Writer's Block is that it is not fatal; it is curable. First, though, you have to learn to identify the disease.

The symptoms of Writer's Block are easy to recognize. It is difficult to make yourself sit down at the computer to work. Your mind shies away from even thinking about your book because you feel uncomfortable or frustrated or maybe a little guilty.

If you sit at your computer, nothing happens. Unlike the day or the week before when words flowed easily from your mind to the computer screen, today there is nothing. Your mind is a blank.

If you do manage to write a few sentences, you are sure they are no good. They don't express your thoughts or ideas, the grammar is terrible, the structure is poor, the dialogue is stilted. There is no grace or creativity in your words.

If these symptoms persist for more than an hour or two, you move to the second stage of this dreaded disease: You begin to doubt yourself. Why did you ever think you could write in the first place? Obviously, your talent has gone, fled to the far reaches of the atmosphere. You are sure it will never return.

What's Holding You Back?

The more I learn about Writer's Block, the more I understand when we are blocked there is usually some underlying fear that is preventing us from writing. No, I'm not trying to play psychologist here; I've just heard all the excuses—and yes, even made some of them myself—such as "I just don't have time" or "I'm too tired" or "I have no place quiet to write."

If you really want to write—if you really have a passion to write about your subject—you'll find a way around those blocks. Sure, you're tired, but knowing you are going to sit down and write about something you love is a great way to overcome that exhausted feeling. If you have kicked out the kids, organized your writing space, put on the perfect music, poured yourself a glass of wine, and still can't seem to write, it's time to go to the next level and figure out just what is holding you back.

I recently spoke with a person who quit working on her book when she was only one chapter away from finishing it. "I just don't know what to write," she told me, even though she had already written eleven out of her twelve proposed chapters. We talked about all the excuses she made for not finishing her book—her husband had a new job, things had been stressful at home, she was involved in a fundraising committee for her child's school. She had at least three or four other excellent excuses for not finding a few hours to finish that last chapter. Finally, I asked her, "What's really going on? What are you afraid of?"

"That's a good question," she said, and thought for a few minutes. "I guess I'm really afraid that the book's going to be a success. What happens if it really takes off and I get the calls to do seminars and speaking engagements like I've always said I wanted? It might take me away from my family."

Eventually, she did get over her fears, published her book, and found while she does get calls for interviews, in the digital age many of them can be done from home.

Finding the Cure

Luckily, most of us aren't stuck with fears quite as paralyzing as my friend's. At some point in working on your book you'll likely reach a sticking point. The good news: You probably won't need psychoanalysis to get over your Writer's Block. In fact, working through the problem may be more important than figuring out the reason for it in the first place.

So what's the cure? Like falling off a horse, the best cure for Writer's Block is to get back up and try again. Here are a few ideas to help you get started.

- **Set a deadline.** Writing for someone who is waiting for your work—a boss, an editor, a teacher—can be the best cure for Writer's Block. It is particularly effective if there is some penalty involved, such as a bad grade, the loss of work, or just the loss of credibility by someone who trusts you. If you don't have a deadline imposed by someone else, make one for yourself. Tell yourself that by a certain time you will have written a certain number of words. Even if you are not happy with those words, don't erase them. Let the work go and come back to it in a day or two. You may find what you have written doesn't look so bad after you've slept on it. It may just need some fine-tuning to reach your usual creative standard.

- **Share your deadline.** Telling someone else you are planning to finish your project by a certain time helps establish accountability. Tell a friend or family member when you will complete a certain number of words or pages, and ask that person to read it when you are done.

- **Do some research.** Sometimes the real problem is you just don't have enough information. You may be missing only a small piece of knowledge, or you may need to spend a lot more time researching your topic before you can write about it. This problem goes for fiction as well as nonfiction.

- **Good fiction is based on knowledge.** Your research may just take a different form. You may need to think more about your characters, find out more about a setting, or spend some time outlining your plot. Once you feel comfortable you have the information you need to complete your work, you'll be surprised at how fast that case of Writer's Block is cured.

- **Check the Internet.** Look at what other authors are saying. If you're having trouble with a lead paragraph, for example, reading similar articles may give you an idea of how to start your own. I'm not suggesting you copy their work, just use it as a form of brainstorming.

- **Walk away**. Take a break from your work and do something else for a while. Get out and exercise, take a walk, listen to music, watch some TV. Just make sure you have written at least a few sentences so you will have something to start on when you return to the work. Set a time to start on the piece again. Mark it on your calendar.

The only real cure for Writer's Block is to keep on writing.

Part 2
Publish

People generally don't recognize how long it takes to conceive, publish, and write a book.

Neil deGrasse Tyson

Chapter 9
What Comes Next?

You've spent weeks and months—maybe even years—writing, editing, and rewriting, and now you finally have a completed manuscript. It's as shiny as a polished apple, and you can't wait to share it with the world. How do you get your work from a computer document to a professional-looking format, the book you've dreamed of writing?

These days you have a lot of options to choose from in the publishing world, and many decisions to make. Should you publish your work as a traditional paper book, as an e-book, or both? Should you look for an agent and try to sell your manuscript to a large publishing house, go the do-it-yourself route, or find something in-between?

The Publishing Myth

You pop your precious manuscript into an envelope and send it to a publisher who opens it, reads it, and cries, "Eureka! I've found the next great best seller!" The publisher sends you a contract with a hefty advance check. A few months later your book is on the front table at every Barnes & Noble in the country, it hits *The New York Times* best seller list, and you sit back and cash the royalty checks as they roll in.

It's a lovely tale, but that's all it is: a fairy tale. The reality is, finishing your manuscript is just the beginning of the process, and it is also the easiest part of the process. You now need to take your book from a document on your computer to a properly formatted paper and e-book with a professional cover design, marketing materials, and a page on Amazon.

Working With an Agent:
The Traditional Model

In the old-school model of publishing, writers first find an agent to represent their work to a publisher. There are hundreds of agents throughout the country, each specializing in just one or two writing genres. Before you send out a book proposal, you should take the time to research agents to find the ones who specialize in your area of expertise. You wouldn't go to a shoe store to buy an oil filter for your car, right? So don't expect an agent who specializes in children's books to be interested in your take on new management techniques, or vice versa. Do your homework before you contact an agent; it will save you time, money, and a lot of frustration. There is information on where to find agent listings in the Resources section of this book.

Finding an agent to represent you is not as easy as picking one out of a listing and hiring them. You must submit your work to the agent, who must then accept your work and decide to represent you. Good agents will only represent clients they think they can sell, and they have many to choose from. Established agents easily receive a hundred or more manuscripts a month. Your query letter and book proposal must stand out from the crowd for the agent of your choice to notice you and choose to represent you.

Working with an agent can be rewarding, and the prestige of an established agent can help get your manuscript noticed by publishers. Finding an agent, though, is only the first step in a process that offers no guarantee your book will be published. I know plenty of people who had an agent represent them who never sold a book. In fact, I'd say I know more people whose work has not been sold by an agent than I have those who have actually seen success through this route to publishing.

I've also known many writers who had a signed contract with a publisher, worked with the company for several months—some more than a year—only to be told that the book "no longer fits the publisher's goals." This means the author is back to square one and must start the entire process of finding a publisher once again.

Just as finding an agent is no guarantee you'll get published, signing a contract does not mean your work is over. Even though you have already edited your book, or had it edited by a professional, and believe it is the best it can be, your publishing house will edit it again, and will often insist on making substantial changes.

Depending on your contract, you will have more or less control over your book. You may have no say in the cover design, in chapters cut from the work, or even on how you yourself can use the book once it is actually on the market. One author I spoke with had to get permission from his publisher to give a seminar using the title of his own book.

Another author told me that while writing a book was one of the best experiences of his life, the publishing process was one of the worst. J.D. Salinger, author of *The Catcher in the Rye*, found working with a traditional publishing house so difficult he finally refused to publish any more of his works. Don't get me wrong. I definitely advocate editing and reediting your book, as well as listening to experts on such things as cover design and title. Make sure when you sign a contract you know exactly what rights you will have over your intellectual property.

New Roads to Publishing

There were many good reasons why the old-school publishing model came into existence. Older printing techniques such as the offset press made it difficult to profitably print less than 1,000 or 2,000 books. Also, there was a time, only a few decades ago, when the vast majority of books were sold through individual mom-and-pop bookstores scattered throughout the country.

To publish a book without the backing of a large publishing house meant that an individual author had to first pay to have a few thousand books printed, then stack them in the back of their car and drive to every town with a bookstore just to sell a few books at a time. What didn't sell ended up mildewing in boxes in the author's garage.

Time and technology have changed all that. Today, new printing techniques and the Internet have made it possible for anyone with a great idea to bypass the major publishing houses and bring that idea directly to their readers, printing and shipping them one book at a time.

Three terms you hear these days that have changed the face of the publishing industry are digital printing, print-on-demand (or POD), and e-books.

- ***Digital printing*** is a process in which books or other materials are stored as computer files and printed on laser printers. The advantages for printers, publishers, and authors are many. For printers, less storage space for old files and less setup time (among other things) have substantially reduced the cost of printing books. This means more printing companies can now get into the game and print good-quality books in small quantities. For authors and publishers, faster turnaround times and lower setup fees make it economically feasible to produce a small number of books at one time. Books written for small niche audiences have a much greater chance of economic success than they had in the past. Digital printing is called "print on demand," but there is also a second definition for print on demand (POD).

- ***POD*** is a business model in which books are printed only as they are needed. If an author is planning a seminar and expects to sell fifty books, they can order exactly that many at one time. If they think they can sell seventy books, they can order that amount. At the other end of the selling spectrum, if a book is listed on a book website, such as Amazon, an individual reader can order one book, which will be individually printed and delivered to them.

- ***E-books.*** I'm constantly amazed at how many authors I speak with who are sure they want to have their book published in this way but have never actually read or even looked at an e-book, or who don't understand the differences between formatting a paper book and formatting an e-book. The broadest definition of an e-book is a book that can be downloaded and read on an electronic device. A PDF can be considered an e-book, and many people do sell or give away books in PDF form on their websites, and a PDF can also be read on an e-reader.

As e-readers have advanced in sophistication, so have e-books. There are several formats for e-readers. Up until recently, the two major formats were .mobi and .epub. The .mobi format was used by Amazon Kindle; .epub was used by just about everyone else.

Yes, there are a few other formats for e-books, but they are obscure enough we are not going to worry about them here.

Amazon's .mobi format has always been problematic and difficult to use. As of the end of June 2021, the company quit using it. Here's an email Amazon sent out to its users.

We listened to your feedback and are making it simpler to publish eBooks on Kindle. Starting June 28, 2021, we will no longer support files in MOBI, PRC or AZK formats when publishing new reflowable eBooks or updating the content for previously published eBooks. Instead, we ask publishers to use EPUB, KPF (Kindle Create files), or DOC/DOCX (Microsoft Word files) files for reflowable eBooks. Please note MOBI files are still accepted for fixed-layout eBooks. You don't need to take any action for reflowable eBooks already published unless you are updating the eBook files. If you are uploading new or updated content, see our Kindle Publishing Guidelines:
https://kdp.amazon.com/help/topic/G79CTKR8BX79E96L

So what does this mean for you as an author? If you already have e-books published through Amazon Kindle Direct Publishing (KDP), you should be fine. If you are uploading a new book to KDP using Word, you should be fine. If you have an older e-book on Amazon that has more complex formatting, I recommend you purchase it and upload it to your own e-reader and check it over. That way you will know if there are any problems. If you prefer to convert your books yourself and not just upload as a Word file, have your book converted to a .pub file before uploading to Amazon KDP. I highly recommend converting to .pub before uploading if you have a book with complex formatting, a lot of jpegs, footnotes, endnotes, or anything else unusual.

I realize that to the uninitiated, what I just wrote may sound like gobbledygook. ***The bottom line: If you have any questions about formatting your book as an e-book, have it formatted as a .pub book before uploading it to any e-book sales site, whether it be Amazon, Barnes & Noble, Smashwords, or another site.***

In addition to new printing techniques, the Internet has also dramatically changed the way in which books are distributed. No longer must the author lug his book from store to store like an old-fashioned door-to-door sales representative. These days authors can go right to the reader through book websites or through their personal or business website.

There are still many reasons to use a traditional publisher—greater distribution and fewer upfront costs are just two—but today there are almost as many different models for the business relationship between author and publisher as there are books in print. Don't assume one publishing model is best for you. Explore your options with several different publishers who offer a variety of services at a variety of prices.

Self-Publishing

Self-publishing has become a viable and appealing option for many authors today. I highly recommend it for many authors. In fact, with Amazon's KDP publishing program, you can publish a book at practically no cost.

I recently had a conversation with an author who was wondering why he would ever pay a publishing house or even a printer again when he could publish his books for almost nothing through one of the many do-it-yourself publishing services now available. Of course, he was also wondering why a well-known, national public relations firm would not take him as a client.

"How many books have you sold?" I asked him.

"I've sold fifty," he told me proudly.

"Were any of them sold on Amazon?" I asked.

No, he confessed, his fifty books had been sold to friends and family through a local bookstore in his small town. He had no other bookstores selling his book.

I looked at his cover: plain, one-color background with the title centered in Times New Roman font. I suggested he make changes to the cover to make it more attractive to readers, but he was uninterested. A more elaborate cover would cost more money with the service he was using, and he was unwilling to spend it.

Yes, do-it-yourself services have a place in publishing and

always will. If you want your book to have more credibility, though, and more sales than only to friends and family, you need to do more.

Self-Publishing vs. Do-It-Yourself

There is a difference between self-publishing and what I call "do-it-yourself" publishing. The Do-It-Yourself author tries to handle every aspect of book publishing from writing to editing to cover design to book marketing in the cheapest way possible. Don't get me wrong, I'm all for being frugal. To get readers and make money in today's competitive book market, an author can't do it all.

To be successful, you must realize you, the author, are now a business owner. You have two products to sell: your book and yourself. Before you decide whether to self-publish or begin the search for a publisher, there are several things to consider.

What Is Your Purpose?

Knowing what you want your book to do for you personally and professionally will help you determine what type of publisher best suits your needs.

- **If you are an academic** looking for professional credibility, you should look for a university press or other academic publisher with a reputation in your field.
- **If you are businessperson** who wants to promote yourself through seminars or workshops and a website, it likely will be better for you to bypass traditional publishing houses and self-publish.
- **If you are a fiction writer** who realizes that often the best way to eventually get that publishing deal is to become successful publishing your books yourself.

Independent Publishers

Today, authors are no longer stuck with only two choices: the search for an agent and giant publishing house to pick up your book, or the do-it-yourself method. There are several basic models for publishing: traditional, do-it-yourself, small independent publishers, and hybrid models.

Assisted self-publishers, or hybrid publishers, have many different models for payment. One model is a "buy-in" in which the author guarantees to purchase a certain number of books. In another model the publisher asks the author to pay for production, marketing, and other services in a package or on an a la carte basis.

Small independent publishers often look for authors who are writing for niche markets. These books may not become the next national blockbuster, but they do have a market.

Let me stress there is no one right way to publish. I've heard of people who were happy with each type of publisher, and I've also heard horror stories from authors who have used each type of publisher. Do your research, not just about the type of publishing you choose but the individual company within that group. That is the best way to ensure that you will have a good outcome and be happy with the services you receive and with the final product—your book.

What Kind of Help Do You Need?

Before you can choose a publisher, you must know what services you are looking for. As a first-time author you probably do not know all the items or services you need to turn your manuscript into a book. Why should you? You are an expert in the field you are writing about, not an expert in book publishing. We'll talk more about this in the next chapter but first, a word about copyright.

What About Your Copyright?

Intellectual property is a complex issue. The registration process with the U.S. Copyright Office is much simpler than most government procedures, and one you can easily do yourself. However, you should seek professional advice from an attorney who specializes in intellectual property law if you have any complex questions or problems with copyright.

According to the U.S. Copyright Office, "Copyright is a form of protection provided by the laws of the United States (title 17, U.S. Code) to the authors of 'original works of authorship,' including literary, dramatic, musical, artistic, and certain other intellectual works. This protection is available to both published and unpublished works."

Copyright exists from the moment a work is created, and registration is voluntary. In other words, it is not necessary for you to register your work with the U.S. Copyright Office for it to be protected. However, there are benefits in registering a work. First and foremost, you must have registered your work if you wish to bring a lawsuit for infringement.

You do not need a lawyer to register your work with the U.S. Copyright Office. All you need to do is go to www.copyright.gov, fill out an application form, and pay a small fee.

Let me repeat this one more time: If you have any questions about intellectual property rights or copyright, consult an attorney who specializes in this area.

Chapter 10
Decisions, Decisions

I have read many writers' posts on blogs, LinkedIn groups, and other sites, and I understand some people often feel publishing houses that ask the author to pay for services are attempting to "rip them off."

Yes, as an author you can handle all these services yourself. But do you really want to? Ask yourself if you have the time and the ability to become an expert in every area of book production. I've already talked about the need to use a professional editor. You cannot objectively edit your own work. I would suggest hiring experts to help you with all the other aspects of book publishing. It only makes sense in today's competitive world of publishing.

If you are an expert in graphic arts, editing, proofreading, formatting the interior pages, e-book formatting, indexing, marketing, sales, and book distribution, then you should go ahead and do it all yourself. If you *aren't* an expert in all these areas and don't have the time or the desire to become an expert, then look for someone who will help you with the services you need. You can find a full-service publisher or consultant, or you can look for individuals who can help you with only the services you need.

Here is a list of items or tasks you need to publish a book that looks and reads both polished and professional.

- Editing
- Formatting as a paper book, e-book, or both
- Proofreading
- Cover design
- Obtaining an International Standard Book Number (ISBN)

- Uploading your book to Amazon and other websites
- Distribution
- Marketing

Your Creative Team

Unless you are a true Renaissance man or woman and an expert in every aspect of the book production process, you will need a creative team to help you. Who should be on your team? Often people start with the people they know: family members or friends they respect. They ask them to read the manuscript and get their reactions to it. This can be a great place to start, but when it comes to developing a creative team, it is not how an author should end.

Family and friends can offer good advice but, unless they are professional editors, proofreaders, graphic artists, marketers, publicists, or publishers, they cannot really offer you the best, most professional advice about your book. I often hear people say things such as "My mother is a teacher; she's excellent at grammar so I had her edit my book." Or "My best friend is a really good artist so they drew my cover for me." I've even had one author call me wanting to make a change in her cover design based on advice from her cat sitter.

Yes, you do need someone to check over your grammar and illustrate your cover, but that's not all you need. So who should be on your creative team?

Editor: If you are using a traditional or independent publisher, you may be assigned an editor. If you are self-publishing, you need to find a *professional* editor. Yes, your best friend may be a really great writer, a teacher, or an expert blogger, but you need more than that. You need an editor to read your book and flag the following details.

- Missing or incomplete information
- Grammar and spelling errors
- Marketability of the work
- Consistent and appropriate style using a manual such as *The Chicago Manual of Style* or *The Associated Press Stylebook*

- Ease of reading and a style appropriate to the audience

I've used the word "style" twice in my list, each time to mean something a little different. On the one hand, "style" refers to the consistency of things such as the use of numerals versus written numbers, italics versus quotation marks for referring to books and periodicals, and other details that, if not consistent, are subtle signs that say "unprofessional" to the reader—sometimes without their even realizing it. In the corporate world you might use the term "best practices" to describe this.

There are several style manuals that can be used, depending upon the type of book you are writing. *The Chicago Manual of Style* is used most often by both fiction and nonfiction writers. While writers with a journalistic background may be most familiar with *The Associated Press Stylebook* (also referred to as AP style), it is not used often outside of journalistic works. Scholarly works in the social or behavioral sciences often require the *Publication Manual of the American Psychological Association* (also referred to as APA style). Other professions also have style manuals. Make sure you are using the manual most appropriate for your book's subject or genre.

There is another meaning for the word "style." It also refers to the tone in which a book is written. A book aimed at an academic audience will have a very different style or tone than one aimed at the mass market, for example. Before you ask someone to read your work, make sure that person understands your target market and the style of writing that is most appropriate for it.

Formatting expert: There are many details involved in formatting a book, from choosing the page size and margin size to correctly placing the headers and footers. If you plan on publishing both a paper version and an e-book, you will need two separate files, one for each. I recommend you create your file for your paper book first, send it to a proofreader, then create the e-book file from that version. There are a number of details, and a few tricks, you need to be aware of when formatting your book. We'll discuss these in the next chapter.

Proofreader: Once your book is formatted, it should go to an excellent proofreader. Good proofreaders are hard to find. They have an eye for detail and a knowledge of grammar and style. A good proofreader is one of the biggest differences between producing a book that is professional and one that reads as if it was written by an amateur.

Cover designer: While many people have artistic friends who offer to create a cover illustration, you will need a professional graphic artist to develop the front cover, back cover, and spine. This person should be an expert in a graphics software program such as Adobe Illustrator, as well as Adobe Acrobat. A cover is much more than just a great illustration. It is a combination of graphics and text that is compelling enough to make a potential reader want to pick it up in a bookstore or click on it on a website and purchase it. A cover is the first impression your target reader has of your book. Studies have shown viewers look at a website for ten to twenty seconds when choosing whether to continue to view it or to move on. Your book cover is one small fraction of your website so assume your potential reader will look at your cover for just a fraction of that time. This means your book cover must be attractive and professional and must stand out enough to attract a reader in less than ten seconds.

Marketer: You should consult with a marketing professional about your website, use of social media, and other ways that you can get the word out about your book. A professional marketing company can help you plan events or seminars, develop flyers or postcards promoting your book, and work with you to develop an overall marketing plan.

Publicist: Public relations (PR) is a complex field with many nuances so before we can discuss finding the right publicist for you, here are a few quick definitions: Public relations is the art of developing a strategic message, and publicity is the act of getting your message out through the best channels.

If you decide to hire a publicist to help you promote your book and yourself as an expert in your field, make sure you hire a publicist or public relations firm that has a reputation for working successfully with authors. The fine art of public relations is very specialized. A PR person who has worked with local small business owners, for example, may not have the contacts you need to get you bookings on radio or television talk shows appropriate for your topic. Your marketer and your publicist should be able to work together to promote you and your book. The best way to find a book publicist is to go online and search. Read several websites, then call and talk with three or four agents before you make your choice.

Too Many Cooks

The last few months before your book is finally published and available to the public can be both exciting and hectic, and because first-time authors have never published a book before, they may feel unsure about every decision that is made, no matter how large or small. Even after choosing a creative team they respect, like, and trust, I've seen many authors give in to the temptation to ask everyone they know for an opinion on every aspect of the book. I'm not talking about making appropriate corrections to the final galley proof. I'm talking about attempting to make last-minute major changes in the concept of the book, its design, or its pricing.

If you've ever sat over coffee with a group of friends and discussed any subject, no matter how important or trivial, you will have noticed for each person at the table there often seems to be at least two opinions—usually conflicting.

I've had authors call me wanting to make changes to everything from the title of the book to its price to the wording of a particular sentence based on this kind of advice. *If you show your neighbor, your best friend, and three people in your networking group two different versions of your cover or two different versions of a particular chapter, you will have at least ten opinions.*

That way madness lies!

Chapter 11
Formatting Basics

The time to make decisions on your book is before it is actually printed—not after. I know that sounds obvious, but I've seen many authors regret something about their book after they see it in print. Do the research during the publication process, not after you have a few hundred copies of your book sitting in your garage.

Make sure your publisher or printer offers you the opportunity to see a printed proof copy of your book before several dozen or several hundred copies are printed, ordered, and delivered to you, or are available for sale through an Internet bookstore. The time to make those last-minute corrections that will make your book look professional is when you receive your proof—so go over your proof copy very carefully.

Even before you receive the proof copy of your book, do some research to make sure the decisions you make on the size and design of your book are the best for you. Once editing is completed you will know how many words your book is and can determine the final size. Every author has a vivid image of her book in her mind: It may be small enough to fit in a backpack and be carried everywhere; it may be a workbook with lots of room for the reader to write; it may be thick or thin, include color illustrations, or be a specific shape. Does your vision of your book work with what you have written, the length of the book, your market, and your budget?

Yes, the size of your book depends in large part on the number of words you have written, but those words will take up more pages if printed as a five- by eight-inch book versus a seven- by ten-inch book, or with a twelve-point font versus a ten-point font. Illustrations, charts, and graphs, as well as various layout decisions, can increase or decrease the number of pages in your book as well.

This may seem obvious, but the size, design, and overall look of your book are, in fact, very important. Size matters. We buy based on our perception of value, and size is a part of that perception. Every author I have worked with is concerned their book will have enough pages to "feel like a book."

When thinking about how you want your book to look, start with a little at-home market research. Go to your bookshelf and pick out three books that you particularly like; they can be on any topic. Ask yourself these questions about each one.

- What are the height and width?
- How many pages does it have?
- What do I find appealing about the cover?
- Why do I like this book?
- Are there things I don't like about it?

Next, go to your local bookstore and repeat the process, but this time only look at books with topics that are similar to yours. They are your competition, after all. How will your book compete with them?

Look for books with about the same number of pages as your work. Make some notes about the books that you see, including the size, the number of pages, the price, the type of binding, if there are illustrations, and whether color photos or graphics are used. This research will be invaluable to you in helping you price your book correctly within your market category.

Keep your research and refer to it when you talk with your graphic designer, marketer, printer, and others on your creative team.

What Size Should Your Book Be?

You can make a book almost any size you can think of, and you will certainly see books in stores in a wide variety of sizes, but certain choices will both decrease your costs and make it easier to be printed by a variety of services. Here are some standard sizes

- 5.25 inches by 8 inches

- 5.5 inches by 8.5 inches
- 6 inches by 9 inches
- 7 inches by 10 inches
- 8 inches by 10 inches
- 8.25 inches by 6 inches
- 8.25 inches by 8.25 inches

In addition, you will need to decide if your interior pages will be crème or white.

If you read the Amazon KDP site it suggests six inches by nine inches as the most common size. While it may be the *most popular* size for authors printing through Amazon, I would suggest it is not always the best size for you to choose. Explore your options before just clicking on "6" x 9"." There are a number of things to consider when choosing what size your book will be.

- If you are publishing fiction, a smaller page size will look more like the standard "trade" fiction.
- Children's picture books look great as an 8.25-inch by 8.25-inch square.
- For workbooks consider the larger eight-inch by ten-inch size.

These are not hard and fast rules, only some suggestions based on experience. You may have very good reasons for choosing another size for your book. One of these reasons is cost.

Printing costs are based on page count. And the difference in the number of pages for a 5.5-inch by 8.5-inch book versus a 6-inch by nine-inch book can be twenty or thirty pages. This can make a substantial difference in the wholesale cost of the book to you, and that can make a substantial difference in your profit margins and your ability to sell your book at a price comparable to other books in your genre. On the other hand, if you book feels a little thin as a six inches by nine inches, you may want to switch to a smaller size to increase the number of pages.

There are no hard and fast rules here. Your goal is to create a book that looks and feels as if it belongs right next to the big name authors on any bookstore shelf or any website page.

Formatting Your Book

There are several computer programs that you can work with to format your book. If you have access to, and knowledge of, Adobe InDesign, you may want to use it for formatting, particularly if you have a book with a lot of graphics or a complicated layout. InDesign is an expensive program to purchase and complicated to learn so I only recommend using it if you either already have it or need it for other purposes besides formatting one book.

Let me say right here: I'm not an Apple computer user. There are many good programs in Apple that I'm just not familiar with. I do know from experience that often Apple and Microsoft Word don't play well together. If you are writing with Apple and have an editor or formatter who uses Word (or vice versa), you may need to convert the pages to a PDF to make sure that you both are seeing the same thing.

Another format that is becoming popular with authors is Google Docs. *I do not advise trying to format your book with Google Docs.* It is free and can be used on notepad and smaller computers that do not support Microsoft Office. If you are writing a text-heavy book with only a very few graphics or illustrations, I suggest you use Microsoft Word, which is a part of Microsoft Office. While I recommend it highly, I will admit that Word is a frustrating program to use, partially because it can do so many things. Google Docs does not offer such versatility, and I'm sure that's one of the reasons for Google Doc's popularity. It may be easier to learn but does not have the flexibility or the features available in Word, such as changing the size of the page. It has limited fonts. I can go on and on, but I'll just say if you are serious about writing a book—whether you plan to format it or not—get Word. For now it is still the standard, and if you plan to email your document to an editor, publisher, and others, you will need it.

However, to really create a professional-looking book, you cannot just open a Word document and use the standard settings. First, you need to make a few changes in your page setup. Several versions of Word are still available (and I occasionally find a very frugal author who is still working with a pre-Windows 7 version of the program) but for this discussion I will assume you are working with Word 2016. Older versions have all the same features, but you may find them located under different tabs.

To begin, open your manuscript and save it as a new file. Call it something like "My Book Formatted." I always do this so that if the worst happens, I can always go back to my original version and know that it is still there.

When writing, many people prefer to work on a book in several files, separating them by chapter or section. If you have done this, your first step will be to cut and paste each of these sections into one document. For the sample document we are creating here, I will presume you are going to make a book that is 5.5 inches by 8.5 inches in size.

Step 1: Open the "Layout" tab at the top of your computer. You will see the words "Page Setup" and a small arrow in the gray "Tabs and command" band. Click on it.

Step 2: A dialog box will open, as shown on the right. Click on the "Paper" tab and set your width to 5.5" and your height to 8.5". Check the "Apply to" box at the bottom and make sure that it is set to "Whole document."

Step 3: Click on the "Margins" tab. Again, make sure the "Apply to" tab is set to "Whole document." Then, set your top, bottom, inside, and outside margins to 0.5". If you have a short book and want to make it appear longer, set your margins wider, but no more than 0.75" on any side. Set the "Multiple pages" tab to "Mirror margins," then go to "Gutter" and set it for 0.3" for a book of up to about 200 pages. If you have a longer book, you may need to set your gutter wider. The gutter is additional space

on the inside of the page, where the binding can make it difficult to see the words. Setting the tabs to "Mirror" and increasing the gutter is the easiest way to make sure you can see all the words once the book is bound. Now click "OK" and your page size and margins are set.

Step 4: Click on the "Home" tab at the top of your computer. The easiest way to make sure that all the next changes are applied to your entire document is to highlight the entire document from the first word to the last.

Set your font to Times New Roman and the size to 12 point Times New Roman is the easiest font to read and the standard font that is used in almost all professionally published books. Also, 12 point is the standard size for text. Once you have finished the next few steps, you may decide to make some changes, such as slightly increasing or decreasing your font size, but for now leave your document at these settings. At the end of this list we'll discuss some options.

Step 5: With the entire text still highlighted, click on "Paragraph" to open that dialogue box. Under "Special" set the tab to "First line" and "by" to 0.3". This sets your paragraph indentations at a standard size. The Word default indentation is 0.5", but this is too large for a small page size. If you are using a larger book size, such as 8 inches by 10 inches, you may want to keep your indentation at 0.5".

Next, set your line spacing to "Single and "before" and "after," which is the amount of spacing before and after paragraphs, to zero.

I know many authors have day jobs in which they are used to writing corporate or academic memos or even longer documents in a very different style: a san serif font such as Calibri, no paragraph indentations, spacing between lines, and additional spacing between paragraphs. However, this is not a corporate document. It is a book. You want it to look like a book. You want it to look as if it just came off the press at Random House or another large, traditional

Paragraph

Indents and Spacing   Line and Page Breaks

Pagination

☐ Widow/Orphan control
☐ Keep with next
☐ Keep lines together
☐ Page break before

Formatting exceptions

☐ Suppress line numbers
☐ Don't hyphenate

Textbox options

Tight wrap

None

Preview

Tabs...   Set As Default   OK   Cancel

publishing house because that is your competition.

Now we are ready for a little extra touch that is going to help make your books look even more professional. In the same dialogue box click on the "Line and Page Breaks" tab. Make sure the first four boxes, "Widow/Orphan control," "Keep with next," "Keep lines together," and "Page break before" are NOT checked. Sometimes you will see a checkmark in the box, sometimes the box will be dark grey or blue. Just make sure the box is clear, as shown in the illustration on the previous page. This little trick will ensure that all your pages end on the same line throughout your entire book.

Now that you have saved all these settings, you are ready to start formatting the pages of your book.

Formatting Best Practices

Before formatting, I suggest you pick up a few of your favorite books (preferably something with a fairly simple layout) and look them over carefully. Here are a few things you should do to make your book look more professional.

1. **Title page.** Your title page should include several things: the title of your book and the subtitle if you have one, the author's name, and the publisher's name and logo. A nice touch is to copy as closely as possible the look of the front cover, using the font and the point size the cover artist has used. The title page is always a right-hand page.

2. **Copyright page**. Use a basic font on the copyright page, a left-hand page. It should include the following details.
    a. The title and subtitle of the book
    b. Copyright©, the year, by (author's name) (for example, Copyright© 2022 by Karen Hodges Miller)
    c. The phrase, "All rights reserved"

    d. The ISBN

    e. Name of the publisher

    f. Credits for any interior artwork and illustrations, the cover artist, and any professional photos such as a headshot of the author

    g. Disclaimers

I suggest you always add, at least, a very basic disclaimer:

"No part of this book may be used or reproduced in any manner whatsoever without the written permission of the author, except in the case of brief quotations embodied in critical articles and reviews."

You may, however, decide you need additional disclaimers if you are writing fiction, memoir, or a book with medical, legal, or other advice. The Book Designer website (thebookdesigner.com) offers a page with a variety of disclaimers you can cut and paste. I suggest you read them carefully, then adapt them for your own needs.

3.   **Your dedication.** A nice touch, but not necessary. If you don't have a dedication, leave this page blank.

4.   **Next left-hand page.** This page can have a quote or a short phrase or be left blank.

5.   **Contents page.** Your Contents page should always start on a left-hand page. If you are writing adult fiction, you do not need a Contents page. If you have a very long book, this can save you a page or two. If your Contents page is only one page long, leave the next left-hand page blank. Current convention says the page should be labeled "Contents," rather than "Table of Contents." Also, all e-books have a Contents page, whether fiction or nonfiction.

6.   Always start Chapter 1 on a right-hand page.

7.   Chapters should start several lines down from the top, at least six lines if you are trying to save space, ten lines if you want to make your book appear larger.

8.   Once you get past Chapter 1, you do not have to start each chapter on a right-hand page. If you want a more formal look or are trying to increase your page count, you can do this.

One final tip for making your book appear professional: the header. Your left-hand header should have the author's name. Your right-hand header should have the name of the book. You can place page numbers in either the header or footer.

Have a Great Cover

People do judge a book by its cover. We have spoken about finding a professional to develop your cover. Long before you get ready to publish, you need to start thinking about your cover; it is the first thing people will see about your book—when you post on social media, put out a press release and, most importantly, when potential readers click on your book on Amazon or any other book sale website. So why is it so many authors want to skimp on their cover?

Recently, an author came to me about increasing her sales. When I suggested she improve her cover, she balked. "People tell me my cover looks much better than the average indie author," she said. It was true. Her cover was better than most of the covers I've seen from independent authors. But looking better than other independent authors is not enough. Your book is being judged by potential readers against *all* the books on the market. It must look just as good as covers from Penguin, Scholastic, or Harcourt Brace. That is its competition. I also know authors who have increased their sales by improving their covers.

When looking for a professional graphic artist, check out what other covers they have created. How do the covers stand up against covers you see in your genre? ***You want your cover to look totally unique and, at the same time, just like the other covers in its genre.*** Book covers for memoirs, mysteries, scholarly books, and romances all have a different look.

Book covers must show well as a postage stamp-sized JPEG. These days, many people are shopping for books on their smartphones. That means your cover will show up as one of several on a four-inch by two-inch screen. Don't rely on a template, a friend who will do it free, or any of the other ways you can think of to get a cover as cheaply as possible. A bad cover will hurt your sales. A good cover will draw people to your book and make them want to find out more.

The Gig Economy

What's the gig economy? If you aren't familiar with the term, it refers to the many people who are working at a "piece rate" without benefits for very, very low wages. *I'm not referring to freelancers who have legitimate businesses.* Whether you are looking for a graphic artist, an editor, a proofreader, or other professionals to help you with your book, please don't use these gig economy sites.

Yes, you may get a great book cover for ten dollars, but you may also get trash. You may get excellent editing, but you may not. I've seen both ends of the spectrum come from these sites. The bottom line: By paying the cheapest amount possible, you are not only exploiting someone but are opening yourself up to other problems as well. The person on the other end of that email may be in Texas or China or India or France. You don't know.

When you look for services, make sure the person on the other end has a good reputation. Look at their portfolio. Ask for references from other clients. Schedule a phone call; don't just rely on email. Find out about them and their company.

You may pay a little more, but as an independent author you are now a businessperson. You don't want someone to exploit you and pay you less than what you are worth. Don't do it to others.

What Is an ISBN?

ISBN stands for International Standard Book Number. If you want to sell a paper book anywhere, including bookstores, on book websites, libraries, book wholesalers, and distributors, you need one. The ISBN is a unique thirteen-digit number. To make things more confusing, it corresponds to a ten-digit number. Sometimes, when registering your book on a website, you may be asked for your ten-digit number as well as the thirteen-digit number, but all the websites I have encountered automatically convert one to the other. I know this may seem unnecessarily confusing; I only mention it because I have had authors ask me about this ten-digit number.

ISBN 978-0-9972024-4-1

9 780997 202441

50999

For all practical purposes, your thirteen-digit ISBN does the job.

You will also need a barcode. Stores require the barcode so that they can easily scan their inventory at the cash register. Encoded in the barcode is the price of the book.

The ISBN identifies the publisher of the book. This means you must be careful where you buy it. Amazon and other book websites offer ISBNs at very inexpensive prices. Many first-time authors purchase their ISBN through these sites without understanding the consequences. Let me put it another way. The ISBN is part of the branding of your book. If you "brand" your book with an ISBN that identifies you as an Amazon KDP author, you lose credibility.

Why? Because Amazon will publish anything by anyone who pays and uploads their material. There is no quality control. An Amazon KDP ISBN says, "I don't know what I'm doing."

So where should you purchase your ISBN and barcode? From www.bowker.com. Bowker offers a variety of "discoverability" resources for authors. I suggest every author go to their site and browse it to see what is offered and what can be useful to you in marketing your book. An ISBN costs $125 for one book or $295 for ten books, so if you have any idea of publishing more than one book, purchase a group of ten ISBNs. You must, however, purchase your barcode separately, and they cost about $50. Bowker often has specials on many of their products, so before you need your ISBN, sign up for their newsletter and start watching for specials.

ASIN vs. ISBN

ASIN stands for Amazon Standard Identification Number. When you publish an e-book on Amazon, it will be assigned an ASIN by KDP. You do not have to purchase it. ***You do not need an ISBN to publish an e-book on Amazon.*** However, you will need one to publish an e-book on other sites. This is confusing, I know, so here's a simple chart.

Type of book	ISBN needed	ASIN needed
Paperback	x	
Hardback	x	
E-book published on Amazon		x
E-book published elsewhere	x	

Your Publishing Name

I strongly recommend you register your ISBNs under a different name than your own, even if you plan to publish only one book. For example, if you are writing a nonfiction book and already own a business, purchase your ISBNs under the business name. If you do not have a business, create a publishing name. Why? Credibility. Your publishing company appears on all the listings about your book, including the book itself. A book that says "written by Jane Doe and published by Jane Doe" will have less credibility than one that says "written by Jane Doe, published by Deer Park Publishing."

This publishing name is called an "imprint." It does not mean you are establishing a separate business. Reminder: If you have any questions about the legal or tax implications, check with your attorney or your accountant.

Chapter 12
Pricing, Printing, and Distribution

Since you need to have your ISBN barcode on the back cover of your book, you will need to think about price as soon as you are ready to talk with a graphic artist about your cover. Since you really can't start marketing your book before you have your cover, the time to start thinking about the price of your book is as soon as you begin writing it.

There are a number of elements to consider when you are pricing your book. Check the market so you know what is realistic. Books should never be priced based solely on the number of pages, although size is certainly one consideration. Works such as highly technical information or items that are classified as textbooks can often command a higher price than books aimed at a mass market.

I've spoken with as many authors who want to underprice their books as I have with authors who have an inflated idea of their books' market value. Before coming to a final conclusion on price, discuss production and printing costs with your printer, distributor, or publisher. Make sure the final price of the book covers the printing costs, plus gives you a profit.

This does not mean that you can charge an unrealistic amount for your book because you have made poor decisions. A friend of mine told me about a book signing he attended. The author was charging more than thirty dollars for a small paperback book. While a few dozen people attended the event, only one or two books were sold. The author's rationale for the price of the book was she had self-published and asked a local printing company that did not usually print books to make up 100 copies. The per-book printing cost was extremely high; therefore, she was charging a high price for each book. Unfortunately, this theory will not work.

Most writers I've met are uncomfortable discussing the dollars and cents of book pricing. They just don't like math, or they have this feeling discussing making money on their book is not quite nice. I can't count the number of authors who have said to me at the start of a book project, "I don't care about making money on my book. I just want people to read it." These are often the authors who give up on marketing first—before their book has had time to find its legs and actually get read.

There is both a science and an art to pricing a product, and a book is no exception. There are very real estimates to be made on the cost of producing and distributing a book as well as on the return on investment. However, there are also other more subjective considerations that involve the perceived value of your book in relation to other similar books, as well as your own personal and professional goals.

There are several numbers you need to consider when pricing your book. If you've never been in business before, the first number you probably think about is the retail price. This is actually one of the last numbers to consider. You must also figure out your wholesale discount, the cost of printing your book, how many books you think you can sell, and the cost of production.

Different sales outlets have different pricing methods and different payment methods. You won't make the same amount of profit on every book you sell, but you have to start somewhere so let's start with the cost of your book.

Cost vs. Profit

How much will it cost you to publish your book? There are a number of items to consider. The cost of editing, cover design, and proofreading should all be figured in. How much will it cost to print the books? Is there a setup fee each time you order more books? The setup fee can be a big factor in determining how many books you order at one time.

Add all these figures up and divide the answer by the number of books you expect to sell. What number did you come up with? If, for example, the total cost of publication will be $6,000 and you plan to sell about 300 books, each book would have to be priced at $30 for you to break even. Not many books sell at this high a price. You are going to have to make some adjustments somewhere. You might try to skimp on the details—do your own proofing, for example, use a "template" cover design, get a friend to edit your book rather than a professional. These are often the first things I hear writers planning to do when they are trying to bring down the cost of printing their book. The other method is to go ahead and charge a price higher than other books in their genre and use as an excuse, "it's self-published." Both of these answers are wrong.

I picked the number 300 in my example for a reason: Because the average title sells between 200 and 250 books. But you are above average, aren't you? After all, you've just finished writing a book. Not many people do that. My suggestion is to develop a marketing plan to sell 500, 700, and 1,000 books or more.

Don't Forget Your Overhead

If you are selling books directly to online customers through your website or if you are selling through any other direct method of selling your books to customers, either wholesale or retail, you have additional costs to consider: packing materials, shipping costs, and the time it takes for you to package your books and deliver them to the post office.

Yes, the cost of your books just increased even further. Now you are thinking that you'll have to raise the price of each book to at least $37. Again, this is backward thinking. Instead of increasing the price per book, you need to find the reach of your readers' pocketbook and price your book accordingly, as well as find better ways to distribute your books.

Market Research

Before you decide on the final price of your book, you need to do a little research. This is actually a lot easier than it sounds. Head back to the nearest bookstore and find the shelf with books in your genre. Look them over carefully. Which books are closest to yours in size and type of information? How will your book compare? Be objective. If all the books in your genre are selling for between $9.99

and $12.99, don't plan on pricing your book at $15.99. If all the books in your field are selling for $24.50 and up, will pricing your book a few dollars lower help you or hurt you?

Let's face it. When we are choosing between two similar products, price is an important consideration, but it is not everything. We want value—the best value for the price we are willing to pay. Books with highly technical information sell for a higher price than books with more general information. Don't necessarily try to have the lowest price. Instead, be realistic about what the market will bear in your particular genre.

Print on Demand

I mentioned the cost of shipping earlier. That was shipping from the printer to you. What if you need to ship a book to a customer? You should certainly charge that customer a shipping and handling fee, but, even so, when you consider your time and potentially a drive to the post office, you still make less per book this way.

One way to get around the shipping and handling costs, the inconvenience of storing packing supplies, and trips to the post office whenever a book order comes in is to use a print-on-demand printer who also offers shipping services. The price for printing and shipping a single book is higher than for printing books in orders of fifty or more, but the convenience factor may make it worth it for you to look into this type of service.

A distribution service that warehouses your books and ships them out when ordered is another alternative to look into if you have large numbers of orders. Again, you must look at the overall cost of the service: How many books must you ship to make a distribution center an affordable alternative?

Direct Sales Make the Most Profit

Direct sales to customers at the back of the room, or as part of a seminar package, earn the author the greatest return per book. Here are some more figures to consider.

Let's say that it costs you $3.50 per book to print 100 books. The shipping and handling from the printer to your office is $40, or $.40 per book, making your total cost per book $3.90. If you sell each book for $10 (I've picked a nice even number for my illustration; many books do sell for more), your profit per book is $6.10. Selling directly to your readers makes the most profit per book but is also limiting. How many people can you reach directly? No matter how often you have speaking engagements, you can only see so many people in person during any given week. You can increase your reach by selling your books through the Internet and other retail sources. Having a variety of ways for people to buy your book increases how many books you sell.

Royalties

Most publishers, even pay-to-publish publishers, have a royalty system set up for books that they sell for you. These can be books that are sold through bookstores, other retail outlets, the publisher's own site, and Internet retailers. Royalties vary greatly from publisher to publisher, and many authors look at the tiny royalty they receive on a book—often ten percent of net—and feel cheated.

"This is my book, and the publisher is making most of the money," they cry. Before you complain too loudly, think about the cost of the printing, the shipping, and the storing of books you are not responsible for when the publisher is handling your distribution.

Working With Wholesalers and Distributors

Another factor to consider when your book is being sold through a distributor is all the middlemen who need to make a little money on your book. First is the printer, then the distributor (your publisher, a book distribution company, or another source altogether). Next is the retailer who sells your book to the consumer. Finally at the end of the line is you, the author.

Yes, the more middlemen you cut out, the greater your profit, but let's think about it in a different way: If it weren't for those middlemen, how many books would you sell? You are paying your publisher and your distributor to get the book into the hands of more people than you could possibly do yourself.

Wholesale Pricing

Bookstores must buy your book at a wholesale price to make money. The problem for many small publishers and individual authors is that bookstores want, expect, and need to get wholesale prices when they may only be purchasing one or two of your books at a time. This is too small an order for you to receive much of a discount from your printer. The typical wholesale price on a book can range from forty to fifty percent of the retail price. In addition, there is the standard practice in the book business that books can be returned and the price refunded.

Let's look back at our $10 retail price. It cost you $350 to print 100 books and $40 to ship them, giving you an overall cost per book of $3.90. A bookstore wants to order 10 books at a fifty-five percent discount, or $4.50 per book. It's going to cost $10 to ship the books, making your cost per book $4.90.

That means you are going to make 40 cents on every book you sell. Are bookstore sales really worth it? I often say that bookstores are the worst places to sell books, but we'll talk more about that in the marketing section of this book.

There is one more aspect of working with bookstores you need to be aware of: returns. It is a tradition in the book industry that books are returnable pretty much indefinitely. This means bookstores are essentially selling on contingency. There are historical reasons for this, but in today's market it is very difficult for authors to accept this method of sales when they know if they sell directly to the public through their own website, through stores other than bookstores, or through websites that use print-on-demand practices, they can do so without risk of returns.

Other Types of Profit

What are your goals and objectives in publishing a book? Making a profit on the sales is just one possible objective. There are as many reasons to write a book as there are writers to write them.

Writing a book can increase your credibility and your visibility. It can bring you more clients or allow you to charge higher fees for your services. It can bring you recognition in your field and interviews on the radio and television—one author I know recently took the television interview a step further: She's now hosting her own show on a local television station and interviewing other people. And finally, it can bring you the satisfaction of fulfilling a life goal.

Your goals need to be taken into consideration when you are pricing your book. If you look at your book as a marketing tool, understanding that you may break even or only make a small amount of money is easier to accept.

Printers and Distributors

Who is going to print your book? How are you going to get your books to individual customers? You have options. Before we begin to discuss them, here are some important printing terms you should know.

- **Perfect bound:** A widely used soft cover binding method in which the pages and cover are glued together at the spine. Currently the most common soft cover book binding.
- **Saddle stitched:** Saddle stitched books are not actually stitched; they are stapled. Saddle stitch is used for smaller books that do not have enough pages for a spine. This method is often used in children's picture books.
- **Paper weight:** Literally, the weight of a ream of paper; sixty pound paper is most commonly used for interior book pages.
- **Cover stock:** A heavier paper used for the cover of a book. This can come in many weights and is also called card stock.
- **Glossy:** A paper finish for cover stock. It has a glossy coating that shines. Some glossy stock will also have an additional coating, making it shinier and more durable.
- **Matte:** A cover finish that does not have a shine to it. This can be achieved by using a dull, or matte, finish cover stock or with an additional coating sometimes referred to as "soft touch." Both glossy and matte are perfectly acceptable for books. It's all about the look you want to achieve.

The easiest way to go is to use Amazon Kindle Direct Publishing as your printer. Note: I said "printer," not "publisher." *You are your own publisher. You own your ISBN and your copyright.* But KDP does an excellent job of printing books and shipping them to you in larger quantities at discount prices.

There are some caveats here. KDP does not sell to individual bookstores at discount prices. If you are set on working with bookstores, you will have to have your books in stock and personally sell them and deliver them. This will make your final profit extremely small. Bookstores want to make money, too.

Ingram: Lightning Source and Spark

Another printing and distribution service is Ingram Content Group, the largest book wholesaler in the world. Lightning Source and Ingram Spark are their divisions that work with small publishers and individual authors. Most independent authors will work with Spark. You must do a larger volume of business to make the added costs of using Lightning Source worthwhile.

Working with Lightning Source or Spark will make your book available through other book retail sites including Barnes & Noble (B&N), Books-A-Million (BAM), and Google Books. It will not necessarily make the books available in B&N and BAM retail stores, but they will be available online.

Before making your decision, explore all the sites, read everything, and decide which service is best for you.

Ingram vs. Amazon

About ten years ago I always advised authors to upload their paper books to Ingram, and to bypass Amazon KDP. After all, if a book was uploaded through Lightning Source or Ingram Spark, it showed up automatically on Amazon, and the printing and other distribution choices were better.

About five years later I found that Amazon had improved, and because it was significantly less expensive than Spark, I began recommending that authors upload paper books exclusively to Amazon unless they were going to seriously go after the bookstore market.

These days, I recommend that authors upload their books to both Ingram Spark and Amazon. Why the redundancy?

1. Putting your book on Ingram Spark gives you access to a wider variety of online book sellers and makes it much more

likely that your book will be listed in Google Books. This added visibility greatly increases your Search Engine Optimization (SEO), as well as giving readers greater choice in where they purchase your book.

2. Amazon doesn't play nice with other book distributors. I have noticed that books uploaded only to Ingram, and not also to Amazon, often show fewer books available and longer delivery times. Showing that only a few books are in stock does not generally encourage people to buy, and showing a book as out of stock is a definite turnoff to buyers. It is easy enough to upload your book to both Ingram Spark and Amazon KDP.

Cost of Uploading and Other Considerations

There is one more thing to think about when deciding which distributor you will use when you upload your book. Amazon KDP is free. There is no charge when you upload a book. There is no charge when or if you make changes to your manuscript. There are charges if you decide to use certain additional services, such as hiring an editor. But with that exception—and you are not required to use any of the additional services—Amazon is free.

Ingram Spark is inexpensive, not free. The cost to upload a book is $49. There are additional charges if you make changes to your manuscript or cover after they are uploaded. This includes change fees if the cover or manuscript are rejected for technical reasons. If using Ingram Spark, make sure you get things right the first time because these changes can add up.

Both KDP and Spark charge for printed proof copies. Amazon's costs tend to be slightly less for this service.

There are a couple of additional things to know before you upload your books to KDP and Spark. *Always upload your book to Spark first.* Remember I mentioned that Amazon doesn't play well with others? In this case, it is Spark that doesn't play nicely. If you upload your book to KDP first, Spark will list your ISBN as "already taken" and you will not be able to upload your book. You will have to contact their help desk, get a lot of run-around, then, with any luck, get an exception made for your book. It can be very frustrating, and it leads me to the next item to think about.

If you need assistance or have questions about anything with your uploading, genres, covers, and other details, Amazon's help desk is great. To access it, click on "Help" at the top of the page and you will be directed to the Help page. It offers a lot of useful information, but if you don't see an answer to your question, scroll to the bottom of the page and click on "Contact us." This will take you to another page that asks you to select the area in which you need help. Then you have the option receive a response by email or by phone. I usually use the phone option unless I need to upload an example for the help desk to look at. Responses are usually within an hour or two by email and within fifteen minutes by phone.

And then there is Spark. If you need help you must email. You will get a "ticket," and within a day you will get a response, and I have to say that I usually find their responses more confusing.

The bottom line on KDP versus Spark: Each has its uses. Before you upload your book to either service, think about your goals. If you never plan to market your book to bookstores, and you don't care that your book is only available on one platform, KDP will probably be fine. But if you think that in the future you may change your mind and want to work with bookstores, or you find that a lot of your readers would prefer to use another site to purchase your book, upload to Spark first. It is much easier to make this decision ahead of time than to try to change it later.

Other Printers and Distributors

There are dozens of printers nationwide who specialize in books and hundreds of other local printers who can help you with part or all of your project, including your interior layout and cover design.

In addition to uploading your book to KDP or Spark, you may decide to use a book printer to print additional copies of your book for you to sell at seminars, book festivals, and other events. Check their prices carefully. They range from excellent to terrible.

Local print shops may tell you they can print perfect bound books but are really sending your project out to someone, which will increase your cost. If you are lucky enough to find a local printer who can print your books in-house, you can save a lot on shipping costs, making this a viable option. If your book is saddle stitched, your local options will greatly increase.

Make sure the books you get from different printers look very similar, if not identical. Paper weight and cover stock choices should be the same whether your reader orders your book online, buys it in a bookstore, or buys it from you through your website or at an in-person event.

There are also printers who specialize in distribution. They will print a few hundred books and keep them on hand at their warehouse, then send them out individually, saving you a lot of time. This can work well if you plan to set up a large pre-order campaign.

You have a lot of things to think about when it comes to picking a printer and distributor. Do your research. Ask a lot of questions. Make sure you are clear about how you want your book to look— including its style, its size, and its price—long before you see that first proof copy. That way you won't be disappointed when the big day finally arrives.

Chapter 13
What About E-Books?

What is an e-book? That may seem like a pretty simplistic question but ask ten people what an e-book is, and you'll probably get ten different answers. The best answer is deceptively simple: An e-book is any book that can be transferred to, and read on, an electronic device. The format can be a PDF or an .epub file, to name the most common formats currently in use for e-books.

When e-books first entered the popular market, Amazon dominated with the Kindle. The device was strictly an e-reader and used the .mobi format. Then Barnes & Noble brought out the Nook, which used the .epub format. The decision is in, and the winner is Kindle; about seventy-five percent of e-books are sold for this platform. Does that mean you can ignore the Nook and other e-book distributors? Maybe. Again, it depends on your goals for your book. For many years I recommended first-time authors use only Amazon KDP. I still think that can be an excellent strategy for first-time authors trying to find a readership. After all, you are reaching the vast majority of readers with KDP.

There is no one right way, however, and I have recently begun to look at another website as an easy way for authors to put their book in front of that last twenty-five percent.

Smashwords is a site that allows authors to upload their e-book free for distribution to most of the major e-book retailers and make it accessible to libraries. The one exception: Smashwords does not work with Amazon. If you want your e-book to be sold on Amazon—and why wouldn't you?—then you must also upload it to Amazon KDP.

Smashwords does provide free tools for marketing, distribution, metadata management, and sales reporting. There are also additional paid services you can choose. Along with distribution on sites such as BarnesandNoble.com, Smashwords also has its own retail store. If you want your e-book to be available through several retailers, Smashwords is the best place to upload it.

Advantages and Disadvantages

There is no one right answer that works for every author. There are distinct advantages in focusing your e-book sales on Amazon, particularly if you are a first-time author. There are also advantages to marketing on several different sites. Your decision should be based on several factors: your time, your money, your marketing plan, and your IT knowledge and ability. There are costs involved in formatting an e-book (unless you can do it yourself), and you must also make sure you track your sales and marketing on both Amazon and Smashwords (or any other site you decide to use).

If you are a first-time author looking for an audience, sending all your readers to one site to purchase your book can increase your rankings on that site, which, in turn, increases your visibility. While this is particularly important on Amazon, it is also relevant to other book retail sites. Amazon also offers its KDP Select program, which increases your royalties to seventy-five percent, rather than the thirty percent you receive if your e-book is available on other sites as well.

I've also found that I can upload a book to KDP using a Word document and making only a few technical adjustments. When uploading to Smashwords, the document that looked great on KDP was not accepted. After several tries at changing the formatting, I sent my book to a specialized e-book formatter to make sure that I could upload it successfully to Smashwords. This is a small additional cost, but one you should consider when making your choices.

The book I was attempting to upload had a lot of bullet points and graphics. I suspect a book that is only text, such as a novel, might upload fine to Smashwords without the additional expense.

Formatting Your Book

Formatting your e-book means first knowing a thing or two

about e-books. E-books do not have traditional set pages. Pages change depending on the size of the e-reader and the font size the reader chooses. As a person with poor eyesight, one of my favorite things about using an e-reader is I can increase the font to the size most comfortable for me.

E-readers also have a limited number of fonts, but some allow the reader to choose the font they prefer. The reader can also choose to increase or decrease the spacing between lines. This means readers have more choice in how a book will look than they do with traditional paper books, while the author or publisher has less. Most e-reader software has a nightlight setting, or the print can be changed from black-on-white to white-on-black for ease in reading under different lighting conditions.

It is essential to the creation of a professional-looking e-book to have an understanding of the e-book reading experience. *The first step you should take before publishing your book as an e-book is to download the free software onto your computer, tablet, or mobile device and read a few e-books.*

Next, decide if you will format the book yourself or hire a service. I know many writers prefer to do the formatting themselves, but if this is not something you want to do, you can hire an e-book formatting service to help you. Take the time to do it right, and read and check your work before you submit it. Just as with a paper book, nothing reduces your credibility and professionalism more quickly than a poorly formatted e-book.

If you have an older book that is only available to you as a paper document, you can quickly convert it to a text document using Optical Character Reader (OCR) software. Adobe Acrobat Professional is one program that has this option. Be careful if you are using OCR software, however, because while it is a great timesaver, it is also prone to specific errors, such as confusing the letters "m," "n," and "r." I've read e-books in which certain letters always appear as capitals or in italics or certain words are consistently misspelled. These are small but annoying errors to the reader and take some of the joy out of reading. Use the OCR software. It is excellent; just make sure you proof your work.

KDP makes it easy for the do-it-yourselfer. Once your paper book is formatted and proofed, with a few additional steps your

Word document will be ready to upload to Amazon, and software on the site will convert it to an e-book. Here are the steps.

1. If you do not have a Contents page in your paper book, add one now, putting in only the chapter numbers and titles. Do not worry about page numbers. Remember: They don't count in an e-book. If you do have a Contents page already in the book, remove the page numbers. Add all additional content on your Contents page such as Acknowledgments, any maps or important tables, and the About the Author page.

2. Make sure you are in "compatibility mode," which saves the document as a Word 1997-2003 document.

3. Start with the Contents page. Highlight the words "Contents," click on the insert tab, then click on "bookmark." In the dialogue box type "ref_TOC" and click "add." Go to each chapter page, highlight the chapter title, click on bookmark, and type in the chapter. *You cannot use any spaces.* I suggest you use an abbreviation such as CH1, CH2, and so on. Go through the entire book, and do this for all chapters and any other content you want the reader to easily locate.

4. Now you are ready to create your links. Go back to the Contents page and hyperlink it to each individual chapter page. To do this, highlight the chapter title on the Contents page. On the "Insert" tab, open the dialogue box marked "Link." On the left, click on the "place in this document" box. This brings up the bookmarks you just created. Select the bookmark that corresponds to the highlighted chapter, then click "OK." The link should turn blue and be underlined if you have done it correctly.

5. Next, link the chapters back to the Contents page so that readers can click back and forth if they wish. Go back to each chapter page and hyperlink back to "ref_TOC."

6. Always check a few of your links to make sure they are working.

7. Go through your document and make sure any references you have to websites or email addresses are also linked. This is easy. Just type the URL (the address for a website), hit one space, and the link should be active.

Now you are ready to upload your book. The steps for Smashwords or other e-reader sales sites are similar. Some sites, however, require that you have your book already formatted as an .epub document.

There is conversion software available that will convert a Word document or PDF to an .epub file. I have tried several and prefer Calibre (www.calibre-ebook.com). Do some research and see which software you prefer. Many have a trial period so that you can try them out before you buy.

Pricing Your E-book

Pricing for e-books has changed dramatically in the past few years. Several years ago when e-books first came out, most were capped at a flat rate of $9.99, which could either be much too high a price or much too low, depending on the particular book. But as competition for e-book sales increased among the bookstore websites, that changed. Prices now vary from book to book, and authors and publishers have control. Make sure, no matter who your publisher is, you have control of your e-book pricing and promotions.

I notice that some publishers, particularly university publishing houses, price their e-books at only a few dollars less than the paper book price. They also don't do e-book promotions. If you have the opportunity to publish your paper book with a traditional publisher, I strongly suggest you attempt to keep the e-book rights, as well as the pricing and uploads, under your own control. Being realistic, you probably won't be able to write this into your contract, but it never hurts to ask.

Should All Books Be E-books?

As e-readers become more popular and are able to do more, the list of books that should not be formatted as an e-book is growing shorter. Readers are more likely to purchase fiction than nonfiction as an e-book, but some nonfiction does quite well electronically. Technology and computer books are obvious choices for e-books. Business books also do well.

Interestingly, while women were the first to adopt e-readers, today the largest demographic is men ages thirty-five to fifty-four. Now that color has come to e-readers, children's picture books are becoming more popular. Since the pandemic, children have become even more familiar and comfortable with reading online.

The question today is not who *should* publish an e-book, but who *should not*.

1. If you are writing a workbook or journal, an e-book will only work if you do some rewriting and reformatting, taking out the original journaling pages or question-and-answer sections and changing the book to state something such as "on a separate sheet of paper write..." In fact, one author I know published her workbook as an e-book on Amazon and was told to take it down. The wording in the email was quite strong. It stated that the content or formatting of the workbook was not appropriate for an e-book and if the author did not take it down, all her books would be removed from Amazon. Since she was selling more than 100 books a month, the answer was obvious. Make life easy on yourself. If your content will not work well as an e-book, don't try to make it one.

2. If your book contains a large number of graphics, charts, or photographs, consider the fact that while new e-readers may enhance these elements, they will not reproduce well on older e-readers. Your readers are using a wide variety of devices, some old and some new. Your book must be compatible with all of them. It can also be prohibitively expensive to format this type of book as an e-book.

Fixed Format E-Books and Interactive Experiences

Up until now we have been speaking about the most common form of e-books, those with reflowable text. Reflowable text means that sentences wrap to the next line and the next page automatically, and as the size of the font changes, the number of words per line and per page change. Obviously, this works best for a book that is mainly text. While all e-books have some interactive features—such as bookmarks, search and note-taking, and the ability to jump easily to different chapters—one of the best features is the "About the author" section, which can directly link to the author's website and to other books the author has written.

Fixed-layout e-books keep the original design and format of the paper book. This makes it suitable for use with photographic books, picture books, graphic novels, or other books in which a complex layout is necessary for the reading experience. However, the problem is that a fixed format book will not work well with every e-reader.

Fixed format books are different from a PDF. While PDFs can be uploaded to an e-reader, they don't have to include the same features as a fixed format e-book and can often feel clunky and difficult to the reader. Fixed format e-books upload easily to e-readers and often feature page turn animation and links to additional materials. When done well, they can create a multimedia experience that is truly unique. At the beginning of 2020 I was working with a nonprofit ballet company to create a book of their version of *The Nutcracker Suite*, called *The Nutcracker and the 1904 World's Fair*. They planned to sell the book as an additional moneymaker at each of their performances.

And then came the pandemic.

It soon became obvious that they would not be giving in-person performances in 2020, but they still wanted the opportunity to have a fundraiser. We created a fixed format e-book with links to a few of their dancers performing sections of the ballet. The book was a great success for the ballet company, and it created a new and unique way for a company of dancers to share their work while conforming to social distancing guidelines. It can still be found on Amazon.

The Nutcracker and the 1904 World's Fair is an excellent example of a truly interactive e-book experience. More and more of these types of books are becoming available, but there are still problems with fixed format books. They work best on an iPad or a larger and newer dedicated e-reader. They don't work as well if you are using a cell phone-based e-reader app or an older e-reader that, for instance, only supports black and white pages. In fact, if you do plan this type of ambitious project, put a disclaimer on your book's selling page about what type of devices it will work on best. That way you will have fewer disappointed readers.

Some Final Notes

The biggest advantage of an e-book is people can find your book, choose it, purchase it, and begin reading instantly. Both e-books and paper books should have a place in your marketing strategy. As you make your decision on creating a paper book, an e-book, or both, look again at your target reader and your marketing plan. The age of the reader, the type of book you are writing, and the type of marketing you plan to do should all be part of your decision.

E-books are covered under the exact same intellectual property laws as paper books. Make sure you always copyright your work, no matter what format you publish it in.

You want to be paid for the e-books you sell on the various websites where they are listed. Each site has slightly different registration rules. You will need to enter your banking information for Electronic Funds Transfer (EFT). Read the directions and rules carefully on each site, and follow them scrupulously, then keep track of your sales and your bank transfers. Web addresses for payment information for Amazon, Barnes & Noble, and Smashwords are listed in the Resources section at the end of this book.

Chapter 14
Audiobooks

In 2020, audiobook sales increased by thirty-nine percent in the United States.[6] Overall, audiobooks generated more than $1.2 billion in revenue. In the same year, e-books made only $983 million in total revenue.[7] It looks like audiobooks are selling a lot more and making a lot more money for authors than e-books, doesn't it? In fact, with those statistics, it looks like you need to go out and turn your book into an audiobook right now, doesn't it?

Well, maybe you do. And maybe you don't. Here are a few more statistics to look at.

In 2020, printed book sales amounted to **750.89 million units**,[8] while "more than **71,000 audiobooks**" were sold in the United States.[9] So even though audiobooks were the fastest growing part of the book market, they are still lagging far behind paper book and

---

[6] https://publishingperspectives.com/2021/06/audio-publishers-association-12-percent-audiobook-revenue-growth-in-2020-covid19/#:~:text=In%202020%2C%20the%20association's%20report,up%2039%20percent%20over%202019.

[7] https://goodereader.com/blog/audiobooks/audiobook-trends-and-statistics-for-2020

[8] https://www.statista.com/statistics/422595/print-book-sales-usa/#:~:text=Print%20book%20unit%20sales%20in%20the%20U.S.%202004%2D2020&text=Printed%20book%20sales%20amounted%20to,on%2Dyear%20increase%20since%202010.

[9] https://publishingperspectives.com/2021/06/audio-publishers-association-12-percent-audiobook-revenue-growth-in-2020-covid19/#:~:text=In%202020%2C%20the%20association's%20report,up%2039%20percent%20over%202019.

e-books. And the additional expense of creating an audiobook means most authors will not recoup the money they spend making one.

Are Audiobooks for You?

Once again, we must look at your audience and your purpose. Why have you decided you need an audiobook?

"My best friend only reads audiobooks and tells me everyone is reading them" is not a good enough reason to create an audiobook. If you look at the statistics on the previous page, you'll have to acknowledge that your friend is an outlier, and you may be making an audiobook that only one or two people will read.

However, if a large segment of your audience tells you they are interested in an audiobook, you may want to consider it. I worked recently on a book whose audience was the visually impaired. Yes, if this is your target market, you definitely should create an audiobook.

Who Reads Audiobooks?

The average audiobook users are men, aged between eighteen and thirty-four years old. They are affluent. They listen to at least four audiobooks a year. They say they listen for both entertainment and information so both fiction and nonfiction books will work for this demographic. They listen while commuting, working, or exercising.

Some Author Comments

I talked with several authors about their experiences with audiobooks. Their results were as varied as their books. One fiction author was approached several years ago by Amazon's Audible to create her audiobook for a nominal fee and a percentage of her royalties. The audiobook has never done as well as the other formats. It ranks in the 100,000s while the paper and e-book rank in the 1,000s. "I suppose it has brought me some more readers," she told me, noting it has not been a moneymaker. It was a good experience overall, because she spent very little for the production, and while the percentage of royalties she received is less, it is "another drop in the bucket" of her overall book marketing plan. She would not do an audiobook if she had to pay to have one produced. "It just wouldn't be worthwhile financially," she explained.

The second author I spoke with has just recently published her audiobook, and it is too soon to tell what the sales will be. She used ACX (Audiobook Creation Exchange), Amazon's equivalent of KDP for audiobooks. She was able to choose the narrator for her book and negotiate the price. She is thrilled with the results and expects it to increase her audience reach.

The third author I spoke with used an audiobook recording service that is not affiliated with Amazon. The cost for the audiobook was several thousand dollars, and while the author is very happy with the quality of the work, she has not seen enough sales to break even on her investment.

None of the authors had a specific plan to market the audiobook; it was just a part of the general marketing they did for their e-book and paper book.

Using Amazon ACX

Amazon ACX is Amazon's audiobook version of KDP. After speaking with several people, it seems to be the most cost-effective way to create an audiobook. It may or may not be the best way. Users can receive royalties of up to forty percent. The website is designed as a "marketplace" where authors put out their requirements for a book narrator and voice artists bid for the job. You can make an arrangement to pay upfront for production, or you can contract a royalty-sharing arrangement. Books can be made available on Audible.com and iTunes as well as Amazon. This is a different arrangement than Amazon has made for any of its other formats. Your book may also be eligible for the new Whispersync functionality for Amazon e-books, which allows readers to switch from reading to listening.

- When working with ACX you can choose your own narrator or "producer" who narrates the book and makes sure that it is a retail-ready audiobook.
- It is possible to narrate your own book.
- Currently, you must live in the United States, the United Kingdom, Canada, or Ireland to use ACX.

- You can choose royalties of forty percent, twenty percent, or twenty-five percent, depending on which distribution options you choose as well as what type of payment you set up with your producer.
- You will receive monthly royalties from Amazon, in the same way in which you receive royalties from other formats.

An Interview With an Audiobook Producer

John Marshall Cheary founded John Marshall Sound in 1995 and built a one-man operation into a leading, independent audio production company. His company has earned multiple Grammy Awards for its productions, which include producing the audiobook version of the Harry Potter series.

A good audiobook is very expensive to produce at about $6,000, according to Cheary. It is difficult for the average author to earn back their money, but there can be some very good reasons for an author to produce an audiobook.

If an author is also a speaker and wants to use the book as a way to showcase their speaking ability, an audiobook can be extremely useful. An audiobook may also be seen as "part of the author's brand," or a giveaway to drive people to the author's site.

John Marshall Media works with authors in several ways. Authors can choose a narrator to read their book. If they live near New York City, they can come into the studio to record their book under the eyes of a producer. If they do not live near New York City, they can have a home recording kit sent to them. They will then work with a producer online and over the telephone to record their own book using professional equipment.

It surprises people to learn that the cost of using a professional narrator to record a book through John Marshall Media is often less than the cost of recording it themselves. That is because a professional narrator is already well-versed in how to read a book, whereas an author may not be. A professional narrator will know how to denote when different characters are speaking just by using "cadence and pitch," Cheary explains, and a professional often doesn't need to start and stop or have long pauses between words and phrases that must be edited out of a final audiotape.

Pricing Audiobooks

The retail price for audiobooks is generally slightly higher than for paper books. Your audience does recognize the additional work that goes into producing this type of product. That said, some of the same considerations you use when pricing your paper books and e-books also apply to audiobooks.

What is the genre? Again, a technical book commands a higher price than a trade book. How long is the book? If your book runs six hours, you can charge more than if it runs for three hours—but not double the price. Go online and do some research before setting the price for your audiobook.

Making Changes

The beauty of e-books is that they can easily be changed. Find a typo? Upload a corrected version. Want to add another chapter? Upload a new version. (No, I really don't recommend this but it can be done financially, and sometimes it should be done.) But with audiobooks, it's one and done. You just can't afford to redo an entire recording because you want to make a change in Chapter 13.

Now that you have learned a few of the basics about audiobooks, should your book be produced as one? The decision is up to you.

Part 3
Market

When you sell a man a book, you don't sell him twelve ounces of paper and ink and glue—you sell him a whole new life.

Christopher Morley

Chapter 15
Marketing Basics

You've done it! Finally, after months or even years spent writing and editing your book, finding a publisher, choosing a cover design, debating over type fonts, suffering through proofreading and corrections, and dealing with all the usual setbacks and delays of a complex project, you have your book in hand. It is beautiful. It is your baby. You want everyone in the world to read it, and you're sure that as soon as a couple of book reviewers find it, you'll head straight to the top of the best seller charts.

Unless you market your book wisely, though, only your mother and a few of your friends and colleagues will buy a copy. ***Do you know how many copies the average book sells? Between 200 and 500.*** That statistic includes every author from internationally famous ones such as Stephen King and J.K. Rowling to the John Doe who sells fifteen copies of his book on the history of postage stamps to his philatelist club.

So how do you help your book rise above the pack and get noticed when millions of individual book titles are published in the United States each year?

Your Purpose—Again

The first step in deciding how to market your book is to look one more time at your purpose in writing it. Yes, I know I sound like a broken record on this subject, and right now you are thinking "of course my purpose is to sell as many books as possible." But is it really? Unless you are clear on why you are doing something, how will you know if you have achieved the results you are looking for? Your purpose in writing your book will be a driving force in how you market it. And, whether you write fiction or nonfiction, you may have any number of purposes in writing it.

A fiction writer may hope to sell enough books to make a full-time career in writing. Or they might want to use their book to gain credibility in the literary world and be asked to lead writers' conferences and workshops, become a guest lecturer at a school, or be offered a permanent post as a professor in a university English department.

For nonfiction writers the purpose can be even more varied. Many authors hope to use their book to develop a national platform for their ideas. Others might see their book as only one of many items they will sell on their website to build their brand or increase their profits. Still others see their book as strictly a way to enhance their credibility with prospective clients. What are you trying to achieve with your book? Think about the answer before you even start to think about the ways to market it.

Ten Marketing Rules

What are the most important things to remember when marketing? The list is as varied as the number of marketing experts you ask. These are my Top Ten Marketing Rules for selling books. I try to keep them in mind while marketing both my own books and those of other authors.

1. **Marketing a book is marketing *you*.**
   You are selling your expertise, your knowledge, and your ability to tell a story and to engage your audience. You aren't just selling your book; you are selling yourself.
2. **The day you stop marketing your book is the day it stops selling.**
   If you aren't telling people about your book, they won't go looking for it on their own. There is no "write it and they will come." You have to give your potential readers a roadmap to find it.
3. **Selling to everyone is selling to no one.**
   Your target market is your "sweet spot," the eighty percent of the market most likely to purchase your book. Yes, your book may appeal to a wide variety of people, but which group is the

most likely to buy your book? What traits do they share? Where will you find them? How can you let them know that your book is available for sale?

4. **Don't be a miser; give your books away.**

   I recently read an interesting statistic. One book given away can encourage ten book sales. This is a very important point to remember. Authors get very cost-conscious with their books; they are afraid to give away that sample copy. Sow your books like seeds on the wind—you never know what fruit they will bring.

5. **Depend on yourself; no one cares about your book like you do.**

   YOU are the person who cares the most about your product. YOU are the person who ultimately must make the decisions about which marketing techniques to use. If it doesn't feel right, don't do it.

6. **Hire experts to help you.**

   This seems to be the opposite advice of Marketing Rule Number 5, but it is not. Yes, you are the person who cares the most about your product, and you should make the final decisions. But you also cannot do it all or be an expert in everything. Hire the experts you need in public relations, marketing, and social media. Spending your money wisely will bring you returns in sales and recognition for you and your book.

7. **There is no overnight success.**

   The media love to tout the overnight success story, but if you really look hard, you'll find years of study and hard work went into most overnight successes.

8. **Don't give up.**

   Pick a marketing technique and try it for several months. If it doesn't work, try another technique, and then another. Don't just try one marketing technique and, if it doesn't bring you the results you want in a week or two, give up. I've known too many authors who do this, then say to themselves, "Well, that didn't work. I guess no one wants to buy my book." Instead of giving up on your book, find a new way to market it.

9. **Don't try to do it all at once.**

   Here is a corollary to Marketing Rule Number 8: There are

hundreds of different marketing techniques you can use—don't try to do them all at once unless you have a large publicity staff behind you. Do some research, pick three or four things you think will work best for you and your book, and do them well.

10. **Always look professional.**

This goes for both you and your book. You wouldn't go to a business event wearing torn jeans and a t-shirt. Why would you try to save money by skipping steps on your book's appearance? Pay for a professional editor, proofreader, and graphic artist. Make sure your book looks as professional as you do.

Chapter 16
Your Marketing Plan

Before you can effectively market your book, you need a plan. Without one, your marketing will feel helter-skelter, and probably bring you very few positive results. Start by thinking creatively about how to market your book using both digital and in-person marketing. Everything from tweeting and blogging to good old-fashioned networking should be considered. One author I know recently sold 200 books in the first ten days after publication using only word-of-mouth marketing and networking in her community. Another author is great at selling her book to individuals with whom she starts conversations in restaurants, parking lots, or on the hiking trail. With a good plan, you can do this, and more, too.

Here is a sample marketing plan to get you started. Put a checkmark next to the ideas you think will work for you. Use a separate sheet of paper to add additional ideas of your own.

__Send news releases to local, regional, and national publications about your book.

__Send copies of your book review websites.

__Have a party. Invite your friends, family, and business associates. Announce the event to local media.

__Have a Zoom book launch. Market it on Facebook. Offer your book for sale in your Facebook invitation.

__Place a book trailer (a one-minute or less video for your book) on YouTube and other Internet sites to advertise your book.

__Blog and tweet about your area of expertise.

__Develop add-on products that sell your book. If you're a fiction writer, for instance, can your book be adapted for a computer game?

__These days most books are not sold in traditional bookstores. Make a list of gift shops and boutiques selling items related to your book.

Now, using these ideas, create your own marketing plan.

Create a Budget

Once you've decided on how to market your book, ask yourself which portions of your plan you can do yourself and which ones will need the help of a book publicist, marketer, or social media expert. Sure, you can probably write a news release that will get you into the local newspaper, but if your goal is to get an interview on a national news show, you will need help getting there. No one starts out with an interview in *The Wall Street Journal* or on a national talk show. Get your feet wet with local marketing, then regional marketing, then go for the national audience.

Set up a timeline and a budget; be realistic about it. Marketing costs money, but it can pay for itself in increased sales of your book and increased recognition of you as an expert in your field. Here are two samples of an easy checklist you can use to develop your own marketing plan and budget.

Marketing activity: Press release for local publications, TV, and radio announcing the publication of a book by a local author

Steps:

1. Find or create a list of all appropriate media outlets in the county.

2. Identify the proper person at each outlet and the person's preferred contact method.

3. Write a news release.

4. Distribute the news release via email and snail mail. Include copies of your book or book excerpts when appropriate.

5. Follow up with telephone calls.

Budget: $200 for postage; copies of book to be distributed to the media

Marketing activity: Hold a seminar on your book topic
Steps:
1. Develop an outline for a one- to two-hour seminar.
2. Find a meeting place to hold it (for example, local libraries and restaurants are good locations).
3. Set a price for the event based on the cost of the meeting place, marketing materials, seminar materials, and refreshments.
4. Decide whether to sell your book after the seminar or include it in the workshop price.
5. Announce your seminar through your website, newsletter, and news releases.

Budget: A seminar budget can be anywhere from the cost of materials to $1,000 or more for an elaborate setup. Use the checklist on the following pages to develop your own marketing plan and budget.

Use the above checklist to develop your own marketing plan. First, choose a specific activity, write down the steps needed to complete it, and then determine your budget. The final step is to make sure your budget is realistic. If you need to hire additional help to host that seminar or write the press release, find out how much it will cost before you start announcing plans.

Chapter 17
Pre-Publication Marketing

You need to begin marketing your book even before you finish writing it. In fact, you should begin to develop your marketing strategy to sell your book at the same time you begin working on the outline for it.

Learn a lesson from filmmakers, who are great at building an audience long before the film's release date. You need to do the same for your book. Start with the people you know, then move out from there. This means you need to start with word-of-mouth marketing—and in this case I mean that literally. Tell people about your book. Tell your family, tell your friends, tell your co-workers, tell strangers you meet at a party or networking event. It is amazing what the phrase "I'm writing a book on…" can do.

A fellow author who is working on her second book recently experienced the magic this phrase carries with it.

"When I was writing my first book, I never told anyone about it until it was almost ready to be published," she says. "This time, I'm only on Chapter 3, but I was at a networking lunch the other day, and when it was time to introduce myself, I said I was writing a book, and I mentioned the title. Two people came up to me later and set up meetings with me. They said they really identified with the title of the book, and since I was writing about the subject, I must be an expert."

As soon as I started writing my first book, I also experienced something similar. At a networking event, I mentioned I was writing a book about how to write a book. It turned out that the person I was speaking to was the program chairman for another organization, and always on the lookout for guest speakers. Suddenly, I was making the rounds of several chapters of a statewide organization.

Word of mouth is awesome. You never know who you are speaking with or who they know, so get over your shyness, your modesty, or your fear, and tell the world about your book.

Another quick way to tell people about your book is to add it to your email signature.

For example:

John Smith

Author of *The ABCs of Growing Cabbages*,

available soon

Keep the date of publication vague at first, then make it more definite as you go along. The phrase can change from "available soon" to "coming this fall" to "on sale October 20," and you can finally add a link to your website's shopping cart or to Amazon.

Your Back Cover "Blurb"

Before you can really talk about your book, you have to know what it is about. Now is the time to create a two- or three-paragraph description for your book. You will use it on the back cover of the printed copy, on your sales page on Amazon and other book sales sites, when you create e-book promotions, in press releases…the list goes on and on.

There is no one tried-and-true formula for creating this blurb. I've seen short blurbs and long ones. I've had people tell me to never start or end with a question, and other people tell me to always use questions. You get the idea. Here are a few pointers.

You are writing a marketing piece, not a book report. Catch the reader's attention in the first sentence and give them a compelling reason to buy your book.

Think "benefits," not "features." If you have ever worked in a sales position, you have heard this phrase. What is the difference? A feature is something the product has. A benefit is how that feature helps the buyer.

For example, if you are selling a refrigerator, the phrase "it has seven different food drawers" would be a feature. "The seven different drawers make it easy for you to keep different types of food at different temperatures, keeping them fresher longer" is taking that feature and turning it into a benefit for the customer.

The same is true for your book. What are the benefits for the reader? It may be easy to figure this out if you are writing nonfiction; for fiction writers, it is harder. Think of your "benefits" as why the reader wants to read your book. Make your cover copy so compelling the reader needs to know how the book ends.

Social Networking

If you haven't started social networking, do so today. If you have a Facebook page, link it to an Instagram page, and start posting about your book. Give your friends status updates on how many chapters you have written. Talk about the writing process, post excerpts, add a link to a pre-order page, and announce your book launch party and other events. These are your friends, after all, and they are on your Facebook page because they are interested in what you are doing.

Are you on LinkedIn, ZoomInfo, or other similar sites that emphasize professional networking? If not, you should be. Pick one or two and join now. However, even if you haven't signed up for some of these sites, you may be listed there. Search your name on several sites to see if you are listed and if the information is accurate.

It's particularly important if you have a common name. I recently checked one of these profile sites and found my information was mixed up with a high school music teacher in the Midwest with a similar name. Most of these sites allow you to log in and edit your own information without paying a fee. Make sure when you are looking over your information you add your book, and, if possible, a link to a website where it can be purchased.

Blogs and Newsletters

A blog gives you the space to post longer excerpts from your book, and it can also increase your credibility and your name recognition. Start your blog while you are still writing your book; it takes time to develop a following and prospective buyers for your book. Send people to your blog by linking it to Facebook or other social media.

You may also want to start a newsletter. This is a little more complex because you must get permission from the people to whom you send your newsletter. You don't want to be a spammer. But getting this permission is simpler than it seems.

I suggest Mailchimp as a great service to use for your email newsletter. It is free. It does take a little bit of learning to use, but there are tutorials. And following its permission process will help keep you from accidentally spamming friends, acquaintances, and readers.

Start your newsletter list by going through your email contacts and adding their names to the list. Collect business cards at networking events, get email lists at Zoom events. If you have a booth at a book festival, put out a piece of paper to collect emails. Your first newsletter may only have ten or twelve people on it, but you've got to start somewhere.

Other Pre-Publication Marketing

As a writer in the twenty-first century, you are a small business owner. You need to delegate the tasks you don't do well and focus on the tasks that you are expert in and that only you can do.

Too many authors I know market their books haphazardly. They start a blog, write for a few weeks, then lose interest and quit writing. They send a press release to five or ten media outlets without learning who they should contact or doing any follow-up. Then they become discouraged when they get no response from the media. They are asked to do a workshop by a local organization and get great feedback, but never send out requests to speak to other organizations—and then wonder why they never get another request to speak.

Do any of these scenarios sound like you? Get out of the rut this type of "start and stop" marketing has put you in and develop a marketing plan for both you and your book.

Get Some Professional Photos Made

One of the things I hear the most groans about from the authors I work with is getting a professional photograph taken. I have to admit I've moaned, groaned, and put this off as much as possible for myself. The fact remains you really do need at least one well-done professional photograph of yourself.

Spend the money, and get some quality photographs taken. Definitely get one great head shot for your press kit and for use on flyers advertising your seminars. This photo can also be used for the back cover of your book. You may want to consider additional "atmosphere photos" taken outdoors or in a setting that shows you doing an activity related to your book.

Do NOT stand in front of a wall and have a friend or relative take your photo with a cell phone camera. You really don't want to look as if you have used a photo from a police line-up or, at best, your driver's license. Do not use candid photos either. Most are blurry and don't reproduce very well.

Do NOT continue to use a photo that is ten, fifteen, or twenty years old. Yes, you looked great in it. And you tell yourself that you really haven't changed your hairstyle so you still look exactly the same.

Trust me. You don't. I've seen too many websites or books marketing an author or speaker with a great photo. Then I've met the person—and not even recognized them.

Every five years update your professional photos.

Put Together a Media Kit

Put together a press kit that can be mailed out to the media, sent by email as a combination of PDFs and JPEG files, and also downloaded from your website. When mailing a press kit use excellent quality paper and, along with your photo, add a link to a website where it can be downloaded as a JPEG file. The goal of the kit is to make it as easy as possible for the media to write about you.

Your media kit should contain:

a. A basic press release announcing the book, which can be adapted for seminars, special appearances, and book launches

b. Your photo and a link for downloading the .jpeg files

c. Your bio—make it one page or less

d. A photo or .jpeg file of your book cover

e. An excerpt from your book—no more than a few pages, please

f. Promotional materials, such as postcards or bookmarks (see below)

Promotional Materials

There will be a two- to three-month period between when you have a completed manuscript and have a beautiful cover and are waiting for proofreading, printing proofs, and finally—your book. This is when you want to really start marketing your new product. Have your graphic designer make a bookmark, business card, or postcard to match the cover. It should include the title of the book, the publication date, your name and contact information, and a web address for pre-ordering the book. Hand these out instead of your regular business card. While I've seen both business cards and postcards used successfully this way, my favorite marketing tool for books is a bookmark. After all, what could be more appropriate? I've also found while people are inclined to quickly discard postcards and business cards, they are more likely to keep and use bookmarks.

Also, ask your designer to include a graphic that is sized for social media. Having an attractive banner adds a lot to your Facebook, Twitter, Instagram, TikTok, and other platforms.

Plan Your Book Launch

How will you launch your book? With a public book signing? With a great party for friends and family? With a media tour? The time to start planning your launch is several months before your book's date of publication.

The media needs anywhere from a few weeks to a few months to schedule articles and interviews. Newspapers and radio stations, for instance, have short deadlines, but magazines often plan their production schedules three to six months ahead. Find out the deadlines for the media you want to attract, and send announcements out accordingly.

Whether you are planning a public event or a more private party, you need to find a location, contact a caterer, and send invitations. Consider partnering with a local business to host the launch. For example, if you are writing a book on hiking, ask a local sporting goods store to host your book launch. Likewise, a gift boutique would be a good partner for any book aimed at a female audience.

You can also contact local bookstores to see if they will partner with you for a book signing. Make sure no matter what type of business you partner with that you make arrangements about book sales very clear. Who will supply the books? What percentage of profits will each of you get from book sales made during the signing?

I've seen all types of arrangements and agreements made between authors and local businesses; the secret is to have very specific, written agreements made beforehand.

What Help Do You Need?

Just as with producing a book, most of us don't have the time, skills, or contacts to completely handle all the marketing for our book or our business.

Once you have developed your marketing plan, look at each of the elements in it. What can you do yourself, and what should you hire out to other professionals?

For instance, you may want to do your own social networking but have no idea how to write a press release. There are plenty of good marketing and communications companies in every community that have the experience, the contacts, and the expertise to help you. It will take you several hours, or more likely days, to develop your own media list. A marketing company already has that information at its fingertips—and its lists are usually larger and more up-to-date than ones you can develop on your own. It may be more effective to ask a marketing company or public relations agency to handle this portion of your marketing.

Working With the Media

Start to research your local media before you are ready to launch your book. I can't tell you the number of people who have complained to me over the years that their local newspaper, television, or radio station pays no attention to them. When I question them on how they contacted the media, however, I often find they have either made one or two half-hearted attempts and given up, or they have blanketed every outlet they could think of with a press release that was so general it gave no information.

Remember Marketing Rule Number 2: If you are targeting everyone, you are targeting no one. This is as true for marketing to the media as it is to marketing to readers.

The first thing to remember about the media is that it is not one amorphous blob. Each separate newspaper, magazine, television, and radio station has its own special niche audience and its own special way of targeting that niche. This is also true for bloggers, online reviewers, and other online news outlets.

Let's take a look at that broad category called "women's magazines." While yes, they all target women, they are not identical. *Redbook, Good Housekeeping, InStyle, Parents,* and *Cosmopolitan* are all magazines aimed at women, but their focuses are not identical. You would not promote a book on childcare to *Cosmopolitan,* but you would promote it to both *Redbook* and *Parents* magazine. I could continue with my examples, but I hope you get the point. So here are some tips for working with the media. They are relevant whether you are trying to get an article in your local weekly newspaper, and their online site, or a national television show.

Once you have a list of media outlets that look like a good fit for you, find the right person to contact at each one. Even smaller news outlets have a variety of editors or reporters who deal with specific topics. Find out who deals with your specific topic. If you are planning a book event, it may be a different person than a general press release about your book. The same is true for contacting television shows. Do not address the press release to the host of the show. The show's producer is the person who most often chooses the guests.

Internet radio shows and blog book reviews are a very important part of book marketing. Do not forget about them in your search for the right media outlet. If they have the right target market, you may get more direct benefit in greater sales than by being on a regional or national show with a larger, but less-targeted, audience.

When people ask me the best way to get an article in the newspaper, I tell them to "get to know an editor or reporter." The same advice holds true for all media. Developing a relationship and some credibility with the person will make it much more likely that your press releases and book reviews will be used.

Don't just send out a press release and expect it to be published. Whenever you send out a press release, make sure that you follow up. I recently spoke with someone who had followed up his emailed press releases by mailing out cards with a photo of his product. He wondered why he hadn't received any response. Mailing information is not the same as speaking to someone.

Follow-up means a personal phone call. Be polite, inquire if the reporter got the press release, and ask if you can give him or her any additional information.

Your Website

If you don't have a website, you need one. If you do have a website, you need to add a page about your book to it. You may decide to add a shopping cart feature so customers can buy your book directly from you, or you may choose to simply link your book page to book selling sites such as Amazon or Google Books. In any case, you will need to spend some money on your website. This can be anywhere from a few hundred dollars to several thousand dollars, depending on whether or not you already have a website and how elaborate you want it to be.

If you've never had a site before, shop around and talk to several different web designers. Each will have different ideas, techniques, and prices for websites. There are also dozens of sites where you can buy a template website and create it yourself very inexpensively. Some of these are specifically targeted to authors, others are more general. At any rate, read carefully about several sites before you choose one. They all have different features and price points, so read the fine print carefully before you choose.

If you are planning to develop a separate website for your book, purchase the URL and develop the site before you publish the book. This way you can start developing traffic to your site, make announcements about when your book will be available, and create a home for your blog.

You may want to use the title of the book or purchase a site in your own name if you plan to write several books. A one- to three-page website is perfectly fine for an author site. The home page should advertise the book, providing the date of publication, the book cover, and links to any other sites you have. Your home page should also prominently display a link to allow people to pre-order your book (which will become a link to an Amazon or other bookseller site as soon as it is available). The third page can contain your bio and links to a downloadable press kit. Your contact information—email and phone number—should be easily found on all pages of your website.

Chapter 18
Launch Your Book

It's finally here. The day you have dreamed about for months, maybe even for years. A carton—or two, or three, or six—arrives on your doorstep, and your book is here.

Now, what are you going to do with it? You want to go right out and start selling it. Instead, plan to have your books arrive at least a month before the official launch date. That will give you time to take care of all the final details for your launch events, as well as send out advance copies to reviewers and make sure all the details have been taken care of. I've been through plenty of book launches where I watched the author sweat it out waiting for the books to arrive the day before the book launch. Believe me, it's no fun.

Let's start by going back over the basics. I hope you've already handled most of these items several weeks, if not months, before your book arrives, but if not, now is the time to take care of them.

Where Can People Buy Your Book?

Is your book listed on a variety of bookselling websites such as barnesandnoble.com, amazon.com, and booksamillion.com? If not, now is the time to make sure these listings have been uploaded and are correct. Maximize your Amazon listing with an Author Page. You can, and should, have your book listed on Amazon before the date the book will be shipped; it's another way people can pre-order it.

You need to write a basic press release about your book. Once you have your first press release, it can then be edited slightly for different media and different events. A basic press release should be no longer than one page. Make sure you add anything that a reporter might find particularly interesting, a "hook" to hang a feature story on. Is the book set in the local area? Does it discuss a local historic building or event? Are there other unique touches you can think of? What makes you a unique and interesting interview?

Also, include your contact information and paragraphs about you, your book, and coming events such as a book signing or workshop.

Send Out Review Copies

I know that you want to start making money on your book right away, but some of the first copies of your book are going to be given away, not sold. Look over the media list you created and decide to whom you should send a full media kit, to whom you will send a copy of the book for review, and who just needs a simple press release.

You may decide to send the editor of your local newspaper a review copy as well as a complete press kit. Regional and national media will probably need only the press kit. Book reviewers should definitely receive a copy of the book—they can't review it if they haven't read it.

Send out advanced reader copies to your friends, family, and fans. Ask them specifically to review the book on Amazon, Google Books, Goodreads, and other websites. For more information on planning this type of book launch, check out the chapter on the 100 Review Book Launch plan in my book, *How to Sell Your Book Today: Focus your book marketing for the new digital economy.*

Host an Event—or Three

Book signings, book launch parties, seminars, and workshops—in person or online—are essential events. Use them all to promote your book in the first few months after it is published. You have just accomplished something fantastic, so celebrate. Some events, such as a launch party where you are footing the bill, can be by invitation only—everyone's budget is limited, after all.

Being invitation only doesn't mean that you should only invite family and close friends. Invite business colleagues, referral partners, and, of course, anyone who helped you with your book such as the editor or graphic artist. Plan to sell your book during the event. Have a table set up to display the book and accept sales;

designate someone to take the money and hand out the book while you as the author act as host, network, give a short speech or reading from your book, and sign copies. Even if the event is private, invite the press, and also send a follow-up press release and photos of the event to local media.

If you are hosting a public event, such as a book signing at a local store, a seminar, or a workshop, make sure you send out as many flyers, press releases, email invitations, or other types of advertising as you can to attract a large crowd.

Event Follow-Up

The great thing about an event is you never know who you will meet or reconnect with—even if, or possibly especially if, it is your own event and you have set the guest list. After all, everyone who attends your book signing or launch party presumably has come to meet you. You may not have a chance to spend as much time as you like with every guest, so have a guest book at the launch to make sure you get names and contact information for everyone who attends.

Follow up with written notes thanking everyone who helped make your event a success. Send a note or email to anyone you would like to get to know better, and, if appropriate, set up an appointment. If you are a nonfiction writer, this may be a straightforward business meeting. For the fiction writer, the goals may be less clear but, again, you never know who you'll meet and how you can help each other along the way.

Don't forget to post some photos of the event on your Facebook page, your website, and other social media, and tag the photos with the names of the people in them. People love to look at pictures of themselves and their friends. It is one more way to bring people to your website and keep you and your book in front of your audience.

Radio, Podcasts, and Television Interviews

Radio and podcast hosts love to interview authors. There are literally thousands of radio shows on the air and online, and many run two to three hours, five nights a week—that's a lot of airtime to fill. Just as with book reviews, you can find radio shows to fit almost any niche market you can think of, and it is often the best way for beginners on the speaking circuit to gain name recognition outside their local area.

One of the beauties of radio and podcasts is you can be interviewed by someone anywhere in the world while sitting cozily at home. I live in the Eastern Standard Time (EST) zone, and I've done radio and podcasts interviews with people based in California and other West Coast states. Drive time for the West Coast is about nine p.m. EST. Now that I'm a "veteran," it always amuses me when I listen to other podcasts or radio interviews to imagine the interviewee sitting at home in their pajamas while sounding terribly professional on air.

Television can be more difficult to break into. There are fewer television stations with less time devoted to talk shows than radio. However, just because it is difficult doesn't mean you shouldn't try. Do more research before you get started. Find out who on the staff actually chooses the guests and direct your query to that person.

Sometimes you get lucky, and the book you have just written is on a topic that hits the news. For example, a book on airline safety that hits the press a few weeks before a major air disaster, or a biography of a celebrity who gets arrested/divorced or dies. It sounds macabre, but let's face it: Most breaking news is often about the less-than-pleasant events in life. If a book you have written relates to a current news event, use it. Call your local television station and let them know you have information to share.

Another good resource is HARO at www.helpareporter.com. Thousands of journalists working for newspapers, television, radio, and Internet sites use HARO to get information and sources for their stories.

When you sign up for the site, emails describing the stories reporters are working on arrive a few times a day. The secret is to learn to quickly scan the entries for reporters who are working on stories in your niche. Then reply to the email with a short summary of how you can help the reporter. Do not give up if you do not find anything in the first few weeks, and make sure you follow the rules of etiquette for the sites.

YouTube interviews are becoming more and more common. Again, the beauty of these types of interviews is that they live pretty much forever on the Internet. Make sure that you ask if you can have a copy of the file so that you can put it on your own YouTube channel. That way you know that the interview will continue to be easily available for you to share.

No matter if your video interview is being recorded in a television studio or from your home through Zoom or another recording app, make sure that you are dressed appropriately (nope, this is not one you can do in your pajamas). If you are being interviewed via the Internet, you may be more likely to take less care in your appearance and be less aware of how to make sure that your background and the quality of your sound are excellent.

How to Look Great in a Zoom Interview

Do wear bright colors and put on makeup, but avoid stripes, plaids, and large prints, which can be distracting on a small screen. Do wear pants—real pants, not pajama bottoms. For the most part they won't be seen, but you still occasionally stand up and move around when on a Zoom call. You don't want to be caught in torn PJ bottoms.

Do wear jewelry, and I don't just mean the ubiquitous iPhone ear buds. But also definitely consider wearing them. They will block out background sounds. Yes, since the pandemic sent everyone home to work, we've gotten used to seeing animals, kids, spouses, and others on interviews. And while occasionally it is cute and charming, it always distracts the interviewer, and the viewers, from the message you are trying to present. So get out the earbuds and learn to use them.

Do smile and make eye contact with the screen. You may be interacting with several people on a panel discussion, only a host, or be full screen talking to an unseen audience. No matter which it is, look at your camera. It will help people feel that you are interested in them.

Don't fidget and wiggle around. Try not to look at yourself and fuss with your hair. Do find a comfortable chair to sit in.

Your background is very important. You are not practicing for the Witness Protection Program so make sure that your lighting is optimum and does not overshadow or darken your face. A strong light behind you puts your face in a shadow. For the best effect make sure you are lighted from the side front. The worst lighting combines a window behind the person with a light behind the shoulder. The person watching you from the other side of the camera will only see the glare of light and can often feel as if they are in an interrogation room.

Think about your background. Bookshelves are always nice, if they are reasonably neat and organized. A desk is good. The special photographic backgrounds that can be used on Zoom are problematic. I've seen some great ones, but if you are only using a free connection, you may find yourself fading in and out rather as if you have a bad transporter connection on *Star Trek*.

Before your interview, check your equipment and your Internet connections, even if you have done many interviews in this way. Just a little preplanning will go a long way to giving your interview presence a more professional appearance.

Chapter 19
Amazon

Amazon is one of the greatest things to happen to writers since Gutenberg invented the printing press. Yes, I really mean that. I know that authors and publishers love to bash Amazon—I've spent my share of time bashing it myself. But Jeff Bezos, the founder of Amazon, has almost single-handedly changed the way the world buys books.

Yes, Amazon rules the market, and it is always more fun to root for the underdog. Yes, Amazon takes a big chunk of your profit. Without it, though, you would not have any sales to profit from. Yes, Amazon is complex, but that's because it is offering so many ways for you to connect with your readers. So no matter how much you hate Amazon, learn to use it.

Basic Information and Specifications

Amazon uses the Kindle Direct Publishing (KDP) site to upload all your books. Until recently, you could only upload paper books and e-books through this site. If you wanted to create a hardback, you had to use other services and methods. Now, however, you can also create your hardbacks on KDP, giving you a one-stop shop for all three types of books. The hardback service is so new that I have only spoken to a few people who have used it, but they have all been quite pleased with the quality of the books.

KDP is only offering case laminate books. These are books in which the cover is glued or laminated onto cardboard; think your typical children's book with a shiny cover. The books must be between seventy-five and 550 pages. The hardcover book option will appear next to the Kindle and paper option in your Amazon listing, making it easy for readers to choose this more expensive version of your book.

At this time only five trim sizes are available for hardbacks.

- 5 inches by 8.5 inches (13.97 cm x 21.59 cm)
- 6 inches by 9 inches (15.24 cm x 22.86 cm)
- 6.14 inches by 9.21 inches (15.6 cm x 23.39 cm)
- 7 inches by 10 inches (17.78 cm x 25.4 cm)
- 8.25 inches by 11 inches (20.96 cm x 27.94 cm)

Both color and black and white ink are available, as are white or crème interior paper. The cover can be either glossy or matte finish. Royalties will be the same as for paperbacks, although printing will, of course, cost more. The upside: You can charge more for a hardcover book.

Uploading Your Book

Go to kdp.amazon.com, and sign up for an account, or log in if you already have an Amazon account. (At Amazon you can use one email and log in for everything, from buying widgets on the Amazon site to uploading your own books to sell to setting up your Author Central page.)

When setting up your first book, it will be easiest if you gather a few things first. The first time you set up a book you will have to fill out some forms including tax information and information about your checking account so Amazon can send you royalties. So have your Social Security number, your bank routing number, and bank account number handy. You must fill this section out before you can submit a book for publishing, so you might as well get it over with and just do it first.

Next, know where on your computer you have:

- The formatted Word document of your complete book manuscript
- A .jpeg of your book's front cover
- The template for the complete cover (front, back, and spine)
- A short description of your book to attract readers
- Your bio
- Seven keywords to describe your book

- Your ISBN (you will need an additional ISBN for the hardcover if you choose to upload this format)
- The price for your book
- An idea on the genre categories where you will list your book

Follow the steps on KDP and upload your book. Plan on spending about an hour the first time you do this. If you have never uploaded a book before, you will be surprised at the number of categories and subcategories there are for book genres. Take some time and explore them thoroughly. You want to make the best choices possible for your book.

You will be asked to set a price for your book. Book pricing is very important, and I hope you have already done your research and have a price in mind based on other books in your genre. However, if your book is so many pages that the price you have chosen is not economical, KDP will automatically increase your price during setup.

Once you have uploaded your files, KDP will either approve them or let you know by email if there is a problem. You can also order a proof copy of your book to approve. Once you have approved it, your book appears on Amazon, and you are a published author!

Uploading your book to Amazon is only the first step in getting people to buy your book. Now you have to tell people how to find it. There are several things you can do to maximize your listing.

Look Inside

How many times have you stood in a bookstore and thumbed through a book before deciding whether or not to buy it? "Look Inside" is offered free on Amazon and is one of the most fun features for Amazon shoppers because it allows them to virtually thumb through the Contents page and about the first twenty percent of a book before choosing to buy it. It makes the online shopping experience much closer to going to a bookstore and gives the reader an easy way to sample the product before buying. Using it will increase your sales. I have noticed, however, books uploaded only as paper books do not automatically have this feature. To make sure that your book has "Look Inside," go to www.amazon.com/sitb to read the guidelines and learn more about the program.

Author Profile Page

Once you have set up your book, you can begin to add to your Author Profile. Start with a short bio and a photo of yourself. You can also add a caption under the photo. It should say something more than just your name, such as the title of your latest book and your website's URL.

Make sure that all your books are listed correctly. Amazon is huge, and it is easy for mistakes to be made, particularly if, like me, you have a common name. There are dozens of Karen Millers out there, and I've found that even using a middle name doesn't always stop the confusion. Check your Author Page often to make sure that all the books you have written—and only the books that you have written—are listed on the page.

Check your Author Profile page quarterly to change and update it to add interest. Put on a new photo of yourself. Change out your author bio. Tell people about events where you will be. If you have written a new book, make sure it has been added to the page.

Becoming an Amazon Best Seller

Every author dreams of being a best-selling author, and Amazon is in the business of making authors' dreams come true—in theory, if not in reality. I've known authors who try to game the system by asking everyone they know to order their book on the same day. Depending on the category your book is listed in and the number of loyal friends or clients you have who will actually follow through and buy your book at the right time, this can work, but this is not really the best thing to do. Amazon updates its lists several times a day.

Gaming the system in this way can get you to the top of the list in your category for an hour or two or, if you are in a small niche, maybe even a few days. If the largest part of your target market purchases your book on the same day, you will quickly fall from the top of the list to obscurity. Yes, you can put "Amazon Best Seller" in your bio for the rest of your life, and if that is your only goal, go for it. As a marketing strategy, though, it will not bring you the long-term sales.

When you list your book on Amazon, you have the opportunity to choose the categories it will appear in. Choose carefully and appropriately. It is more important to be listed in the best category for potential customers to find your book than it is to be listed in a tiny category so you can attempt to become an Amazon best seller.

Let's take a quick look at how the Amazon ranking system works. If you've bought a book on Amazon in the past, you may have noticed the Amazon Ranking on the book's detail page. We'll use a frequently purchased book, Strunk and White's *The Elements of Style,* as our example. On the day I consulted it, this book had an Amazon Ranking of 451. That ranking is calculated per hour using Amazon's proprietary algorithm, which compares sales of that book to all other books sold on the site within that hour window. What does that mean for the book's ranking? In all honesty, not much; the only thing you really know is that in that hour, *The Elements of Style* was in 451st place for the number of sales in its category.

Instead of creating a strategy to place your book at the top of the best seller list for one day, develop a long-term marketing plan to slowly and steadily increase your rankings and sales over time. I discuss long-term marketing strategies in greater detail in *How to Sell Your Book Today*.

Reviews

When readers choose a book on Amazon, particularly one from an author they are unfamiliar with, they are likely to be influenced by other peoples' opinions and reviews. Having reviews (preferably favorable, of course) on your book page will increase the likelihood that it will be purchased. Give yourself an initial goal of obtaining ten reviews, because this number will make it easier to get placement on e-book promotion sites.

Do not wait for your friends and relatives to decide to review your book. If they are not authors themselves, they do not know the importance of placing a review on Amazon. You will have to ask. You will have to twist arms. You will have to help them write reviews. One of the most common questions I hear from authors is, "How can I get my friends to review my book?"

First, when posting on Facebook or other social media about

your book, ask your friends to post a review. Next, pick a few close friends and ask politely, but very pointedly, for them to purchase the book and review it. It is unclear if the reader must have purchased the book on Amazon to post a review. I've seen reviews taken down that were from unverified purchasers, and others left up. It is one of those great Amazon mysteries. However, the reviewer must have an Amazon account and have purchased things on Amazon to leave a review. (Yes, there are a few people left in the country who don't have Amazon accounts.) I recently asked a friend to review a book; it turns out she has never purchased anything on Amazon. Here's the email she got from Amazon.

"To submit reviews, customers must make a minimum amount of valid debit or credit card purchases. Prime subscriptions and promotional discounts don't qualify towards the purchase minimum."

Amazon does place the phrase "Verified Purchaser" next to reviews from Amazon purchasers. If you have an e-book, ask your friends to spend the $2.99 or so and purchase your book as an e-book to help ensure their review will be used.

Now comes the hard part: getting your friends and loved ones to sign into Amazon and post a review. After you have asked nicely once or twice, it's time for strong-arm tactics. Polite strong-arm tactics, of course. Many people have a strange fear of posting a review. Some people worry it will make them more open to hacking and other Internet privacy problems. If your friend expresses these concerns, move on. Find someone else to review your book. If they have told you they will do it, but have not, I suggest this remedy: Invite them to your home or out to dinner. Make sure you have a computer or smartphone with you. Hand them your electronic device. Ask them to sign into their Amazon page and walk them through the process.

Yes, I'm serious. It works. I've done it. The steps for posting the review are easy, and it is hard to turn down someone who just gave you dinner.

If someone tells you they have tried to review your book on Amazon and were not able to, ask them not to give up, but to try to post a review on another site. A review on Goodreads, Google Books, or other websites also has value.

Amazon Review Myths

I constantly have authors telling me things they have heard about why certain reviews are taken down by Amazon. I see as many examples of reviews that stay up with these problems as I do reviews that are taken down. Amazon seems to be very arbitrary in how reviews are listed. Here are a few things that can cause a review to be deleted by Amazon.

1. **Unverified purchase.** If a review has "Verified Purchase" next to it you know the reviewer purchased the book, and presumably read it. I've heard of reviews that were not verified being taken down by Amazon, but I know of reviews used by Amazon that are not verified. Asking your reviewer to purchase an e-book (I suggest e-books because they are less expensive) on Amazon increases the chances it will be posted.

2. **Reviews by relatives.** I often hear people say Amazon will delete reviews by relatives. I know of at least one review that was posted a few years ago and is still up that starts with the words: "Proud husband of the author." The question is, how can Amazon know who you are related to? If your last name is uncommon, that might be a reason. In my case, it hasn't been a problem.

3. **Connection to the author.** If Amazon decides you have a "business connection" to an author, they will not allow you to review that book. For example, I cannot review books by authors I work with.

The best suggestion I have is this: Don't worry too much about it. Ask everyone you know to write a review. This way if one or two are taken down, you will still have plenty of reviews.

There are a couple of big "don'ts" in obtaining reviews.

- *Do NOT pay someone for an Amazon review.*
- *Do not trade reviews.*

I think the problem with paying someone is obvious. Trading reviews with other authors, however, needs some explanation. Many people join author groups and websites to gain readers and reviews for their books. There is nothing wrong with this. However, when you say, "If you review my book, I'll review yours," things can get very tricky. What if you don't like the other author's book? What if they don't like yours?

You *can* give away your books and ask for "a fair and honest review." This gives the reviewer the option to click less than five stars or give a less than complimentary statement about your book.

Let me make my policies on reviews clear.

1. When asking good friends or relatives for reviews, be politely assertive. Do everything possible to make them sit down and actually review the book.
2. When asking strangers and other authors for reviews, be careful you do not put yourself in a situation in which you must give another author a dishonest review.

Amazon's Kindle Vella

Vella is Amazon's new way for authors to bring their books to readers. It quietly rolled out in July 2021. In fact, it rolled out so quietly that a lot of readers don't even know it exists yet.

So, what exactly is Kindle Vella? And how can authors use it?

Vella is a story subscription service that lets authors bring their stories to readers in a serialized form, written specifically for the platform. Think of it as a television series—a cross between a traditional network show that releases weekly and a Netflix series that "drops" all at once. Or, for the more literary-minded, it is harking back to older days of literature when authors such as Jane Austin or Jules Verne released their books a chapter at a time in newspapers and magazine.

So, is Vella right for you as an author?

How Vella Works

Vella currently is only available in the United States. It can be difficult to find if you are searching for it on Amazon. It can be found most easily on your Kindle Library page. Of course, you cannot buy books directly through the Kindle Library page; you must go to the Amazon website. (This is a very strange decision on the part of Amazon that I will never understand.)

When checking on the current state of finding a Vella book before writing about it, I went to amazon.com, typed "Vella" into the search feature, and came up with: (A) "Did you mean bella" (B) several books with Bella in the title, and (C) a small section at the top of the page to take me to the Amazon Vella page.

Vella requires readers to purchase tokens to buy chapters. The price for tokens is roughly two dollars for every 20,000 words. The price for tokens varies with the amount you buy, and *you can claim 200 free tokens when you first begin to use Vella.*

The first three chapters an author puts up for a book on Vella must be free. Consider them a "loss leader" designed to give readers a taste of the story and see if they like it enough to pay for the rest of the story.

Now for the Good News

There aren't a lot of authors on this platform yet, so breaking through as an unknown author should be easier. It is easy for readers to give a quick "thumbs-up" to authors and stories they like—a lot easier than placing a review on Amazon. This means that you shouldn't have to nag your readers quite so much for reviews—although reminding your readers at the end of a chapter to give you a thumbs-up is still a good thing. Writers can also leave notes at the end of a chapter giving a teaser for what is coming next.

Royalties are good—fifty percent. But at two dollars per 20,000 words, you'll have to write a lot to really make money with Vella. But more importantly, to give authors an incentive to publish on Vella, Amazon is currently offering a Kindle Vella bonus, although we don't know how long this will last.

As of late 2021, all authors who publish on Vella will receive a bonus based on customer activity such as redemption of free and paid tokens, "Faves," and "Follows." This bonus is listed on the Kindle Vella dashboard (which is a different dashboard than the e-book/paperback dashboard) around the fifteenth of each month. Bonuses are paid approximately sixty days after the end of the month in which it was earned. Additional compensation was paid for episodes unlocked by readers using the free tokens given to readers by Amazon.

This means that compensation for chapters read on Vella is currently much higher than for e-books or paper books. Amazon notes, "Our Kindle Vella bonus program is ongoing. Look for monthly updates on bonus amounts in the KDP Community." This means that it may change at any time. But Vella authors I have spoken to are currently very pleased with the compensation they are receiving from publishing through this platform.

How to Write for Vella

Writing for Vella is different than writing a book. One of the first differences is that since you only need to upload a few chapters at a time, you can start to publish before your book is finished. This means that while writing you need to think in chapters, or episodes as Amazon calls them. Chapters must be from 600 to 5,000 words long. Chapters should have short, catchy titles that encourage the reader to find out what happens next. You can't just use chapter numbers; they just won't work with this format.

If you are a writer who has already mastered the knack of ending each chapter on a page-turner, you are one step ahead. This style will work better than just chopping a book into pieces and placing it on Vella. That said, if you already have a book that is almost complete, Vella might be a good place for it.

Chapters don't have to be available all at once, but on a daily or weekly basis. That said, it is best to have a good number of chapters ready before you upload, just to give yourself a buffer. Readers don't want to get right to the climax, then have to wait three months for the next chapter to drop. Consistency is the key to keeping your readers coming back for more installments. Make sure you always drop a new chapter each week, preferably on the same day of the week.

Covers are different on Vella. They are only a small circular illustration, with the other information above and below it. This doesn't mean that you should ignore your cover, however. You need one great image to really grab the reader's attention and make them want to find out more.

Is Vella Right for You?

Vella could be a great place for you if you:

1. Have a new book that you want to showcase. Don't put a later book in a series on Vella if the first book is already published as a paper book and/or an e-book.

2. You have a "companion book" that can draw new readers to your main books that are already published traditionally. Think prequels and stories that expand on minor characters.

3. Vella is particularly good for genre fiction such as mysteries and sci-fi/fantasy. Maybe even romance.

4. Right now, books on Vella *cannot* be published anywhere else. You cannot take a previously published work and also turn it into a Vella book. However, once you have completed a book on Vella, if you wait for thirty days, you *can* then publish it as an e-book and/or paperback.

Chapter 20
Ingram Spark

If you have uploaded your book to Amazon, why do you need Ingram Spark? And conversely, if you have uploaded to Ingram Spark, why do you need Amazon?

As I mentioned in Chapter 12, there are good reasons to choose one over the other, or to choose to use both.

Putting your book on Ingram Spark gives you access to a wider variety of online book sellers and makes it much more likely that your book will be listed in Google Books. This added visibility greatly increases your Search Engine Optimization (SEO), as well as giving readers greater choice in where they purchase your book.

Amazon, however, doesn't play nice with other book distributors. I have noticed that books uploaded only to Ingram, and not also to Amazon, often show fewer books available and longer delivery times. Showing that only a few books in stock does not generally encourage people to buy, and showing a book as out of stock is a definite turnoff to buyers. It is easy enough to upload your book to both Ingram Spark and Amazon KDP. Here are a few tips for using Ingram Spark. I have mentioned some of these tips in previous chapters, but I felt it was worthwhile to write it again here.

1. You must create your account on Ingram Spark twenty-four to forty-eight hours before you plan to upload your first book so that your account can be verified.
2. If you plan to use both Ingram Spark and Amazon KDP, make sure you upload to Spark first. If you upload your book to KDP first, Spark will tell you that your ISBN has already been used so you will be unable to upload to Spark without a lot of back

and forth emails to their customer service desk.

3. Be aware of the fees that Ingram Spark charges. It costs $49 to upload a print book only, or both a print and an e-book. It costs $25 to upload only an e-book on Ingram Spark. *If you make any changes to a print book, there is a $25 fee per change.* This is one of the biggest differences between Spark and KDP and is very important to be aware of. Change fees are charged once you have completely uploaded the book, even if you have not yet accepted it. It can become costly so make sure your templates, margins, and other details are correct before you upload.

4. The site can be tricky to use. It has a bad habit of not accepting information you copy and paste until you close out of the site and log back in. I'm not sure why; I've just found that if I get an error message, it usually clears itself if I do this.

5. There are a number of free resources including a weekly blog, a podcast, and downloadable guides. If you plan to use the site, definitely use the resources. You can learn a lot of information about publishing in general and Ingram Spark in particular.

6. While the site promises 24/7 customer support, I've found that the support is not as good as Amazon. Contacting customer support by phone is usually difficult, and I've found the email support to often be less than helpful.

7. Your book will be uploaded to Barnes & Noble, Google Books, and many more (the site says it uploads to 40,000 retailers and libraries) but usually the library upload is not automatic. You may have to pay extra for your book to be listed in a catalog aimed at librarians.

8. Until recently, Ingram Spark was the only way to upload a hardback book to Amazon, Barnes & Noble, and others book sellers. Now that Amazon is offering this service, that is no longer true. However, right now Amazon KDP is only offering case laminate hardcover books. Spark offers both case laminate and clothbound books with either glossy or matte jackets.

9. Don't assume that the templates you download from Amazon KDP and Ingram Spark are interchangeable. They are not. Slight variations in paper mean that spine sizes can change. You must download the proper templates and use them for each site.

Chapter 21
Use Reviews
to Promote Your Book

While Amazon customer reviews are important, there are also many other aspects of getting reviews for your book. Traditional book reviews—those long, thoughtful, critical, *The New York Times*-style reviews and "blurbs;" customer reviews on other sites such as Goodreads; and short reviews or testimonials at the front of your book or on the cover—are all excellent ways to bring your book to the attention of a new audience.

The more people who review your book, the greater exposure it has to new and different people who are potential customers. Do not underestimate the power of these types of reviews. Think of them as a form of peer pressure. We are all influenced by what other people are wearing, buying, or talking about.

I know a lot of you just turned your noses up at that idea. "I don't care what other people think. I make my own decisions," you said to yourself. Think again. Do you check *Consumer Reports* before purchasing a large ticket item? Do you ask your friends for recommendations when you need to find a doctor, dentist, or car mechanic? Have you ever bought a book because you heard other people talking about it? Yes, you are influenced by what other people think. That's why getting your book reviewed is an important technique in selling it.

Pre-Publication Reviews

It's a great idea to have some reviews or testimonials before you publish your book. Who should you ask to give you these reviews?

The most influential people that you know who are in your field. A review from an unknown person is much less impressive in this case than a review from someone with some credentials. A review from someone whose expertise is totally unrelated to your topic, particularly if it is technical in nature, is also fairly meaningless.

Once again, think about your target market. Who is considered a leader in their eyes? If you are writing a book about health care, get a leading doctor to write a review. If you are writing a book with a regional influence such as a history of your town or region, ask the head of a local museum to write a review. You get the idea.

Don't Be Afraid; Just Ask

I've spent more hours coaxing writers into asking their heroes for reviews than I can count. "He won't review my book. He's so much more important than I am." That's the line I often hear. It's amazing, though, how many times a simple email asking for a review is answered in the positive.

When you ask, however, make sure you give a deadline date. Even the most well-intentioned person will put things off.

Sometimes the reviewer will ask you to send something specific (three chapters, for instance) or a paper copy. If no special requests are made, the easiest thing to send is a clean final draft of your book in PDF form. Make sure it is the most complete and error-free copy possible. Have the manuscript checked by a proofreader before you send it to someone to review. A manuscript filled with typos and mistakes won't make a great impression. If this is not the final draft, make that clear to the reviewer.

Where and When to Use Reviews

Of course, you'll want to put a couple of great reviews on the back cover of your book and, if you have gathered enough of them, on the first page as well. You may need to shorten the reviews to just a sentence or two to get them to fit. You can also put lengthier reviews on your website, use them in press releases about your book, and add them to your Author Page on Amazon.

Amazon Reviews

We discussed Amazon reviews previously, but they are important enough to mention again. This is where you can call on your friends and relatives. Ask everyone you know who reads your book to add a review on Amazon. Good reviews matter. People do read them, and they do influence the decision to buy.

Do not just count on random reviews from unknown people who have purchased your book on Amazon. Send copies of your book and request reviews from potential reviewers on Amazon's Top Reviewers list (http://www.amazon.com/review/top-reviewers). Once again, look for people who review books similar to yours. If you are writing historical fiction, don't look for a reviewer who only reviews mysteries. If you are writing a how-to craft book, don't target the business book reviewer. Of course, you have no control over what a reviewer says. You may get a bad review; it's just one of the chances you take as an author.

Give and You Shall Receive

Take the time to review other people's books. Why? Well, first, it is just a thoughtful thing to do. If you like the book, write about it. Second, it is one more way to get your name out there. Put reviews on Amazon. Write reviews on blogs and other public forums where you can add the title of your book and a URL to your website to your signature.

Send Out Review Copies of Your Book

As soon as you receive copies of your book, send them to reviewers. Figure at least the first fifty books you receive will be given away, not sold. Yes, this hurts. You have just spent a lot of money publishing your book, and you want to start earning it back right away. But remember Marketing Rule Number 4: Every copy of your book that you give away results in approximately ten additional sales. Send out review copies as soon as possible. A new book is news; a six-month-old book is not.

Where to Find Reviewers

There are dozens of blogs on the Internet that focus just on book reviews. Some major newspapers and magazines still have book review columns, and there are also radio shows—on the air and on the Internet—devoted to books. Once again, figure out who your tribe reads. Are there blogs aimed at your target audience? Send those bloggers copies of your book.

Some authors now distribute complimentary review copies of their books through at least two online sites: goodreads.com and librarything.com. You can ask—not demand—reviewers who receive a copy of the book to post a review at Amazon as well as on the site where they received the book. Some reviewers will do this, others will not.

Journal Reviews

There are also book review journals that are read by librarians and bookstore managers. These people make a lot of their purchasing decisions based on reviews in these journals. Unless you have a major publisher behind you, however, it can be difficult to get your book reviewed in these journals unless you pay for a review. While it is certainly a legitimate marketing technique, it is difficult to accomplish for the average author. If your time is unlimited, it could pay off. But if you are juggling a full-time career and a family, this should not make your top ten list of marketing strategies to try.

Paid Reviews

There are probably more differing opinions on the value of the paid review than there are journals that place them. *Publishers Weekly* now publishes paid reviews as well as unpaid reviews. Another is *Kirkus Reviews,* one of the biggest reviewers for independent authors. I know several authors who have had excellent results with paid reviews in *Midwest Book Reviews.*

Paid reviews may have less value than unpaid reviews, but they do still have value. If you are a first-time author, a paid review may be your best chance to get in front of buyers for libraries, bookstores, and other retail outlets. Once again, there is a downside. There is no guarantee a paid reviewer will give your book a good review. It is the only way reviewers and review journals can maintain their credibility, but it also makes this marketing technique a little bit chancy.

Dealing With Negative Reviews

Negative reviews happen. No matter how wonderful your book is, there is someone who will not like it. If they write about it, it can hurt your sales. But there is good news. One or two negative reviews among a group of positive ones will not hurt sales too badly. Reasonable people understand no one can please everyone all the time.

It is difficult, if not impossible, to remove a negative review from the Internet. Even if it is removed, you can never remove the negative impression it made in the minds of potential readers. Most blog sites do have policies against abuse and will take down reviews that are malicious or inappropriate. Amazon, for instance, requires reviewers to critique the book rather than express opinions about the author or other unrelated topics. According to its policies, it will delete a review that is "illegal, obscene, threatening, defamatory, invasive of privacy, infringing of intellectual property rights, or otherwise injurious to third parties." If you feel a review of your book falls into one of these categories, you can make a request with the Community Help department to have the review taken down at community-help@amazon.com.

Ask for Reviews

Who would you like to review your book? Do you have friends, acquaintances, networking contacts, and others who have made a name for themselves in your field? Ask them to review your book before it is published. These blurbs can be used on the back cover of the book, or just before or just after the title page. You should also place them on your website.

Don't be shy. Think of the most well-known people in your field and approach them. If you aren't personally acquainted with them, try to get an introduction through a mutual acquaintance. If you are in the same field, you may want to reference a trade organization or other connection that you share. What's the worst that can happen? The person will say no to you, and you will move on to the next one on your list.

To ask for a review, send an email explaining exactly what you want—a two- or three-sentence review of the book is just fine, and in fact, anything over one paragraph can be difficult to place in your book. It is also polite to add a link to a reviewer's website or reference the person's work when you print the review.

For example, identify the author of the review as "Antoinette Brown, author of *The Poor Man's Guide to Great Wines*, www.poormanswine.biz."

Attach a PDF of your book, making sure that it is edited and proofread before you send it. If you are just sending an excerpt, make sure that you explain this; but again, only send edited and proofread material. You want to make a great impression, and you can't do that with unfinished copy or one that has errors.

Give the reviewer a date to return the review. Even the most responsible and well-intentioned people will procrastinate. Don't forget to send a thank-you note when you receive the review, and make sure you send the reviewer a complimentary copy of the book when it is published.

Chapter 22
Marketing Your E-Book

Today, the least expensive way for authors to develop an audience beyond the reach of their immediate circle of friends or clients is e-book marketing.

The initial start-up costs for producing a great e-book are the same as for a paper book (editing, proofreading, cover design, and formatting). If you only plan to publish as an e-book, you may not need an ISBN. Amazon will assign you an ASIN, or Amazon Standard Identification Number. Smashwords and some of the other services *do* require an ISBN. Once you get to production, the cost is negligible. There is no cost to upload the book to the various selling sites. There is no cost to print the book. There is no cost to ship the book. Best of all, there are inexpensive ways to get the word out about your book to literally thousands of readers at one time.

There are several sites on which you can upload and sell your e-book including:

- Amazon
- Barnes & Noble
- Kobo
- Smashwords
- Apple Books
- Google Books

We are going to start with Amazon Kindle Direct Publishing, specifically the Kindle Select plan. Once you have mastered KDP, the other sites are all similar. I do suggest that if you are a first-time author you start your e-book marketing with the Kindle Select plan. Why? ***Currently approximately seventy-five percent of all e-book*** *sales are through Amazon Kindle.* If you want to make a name for yourself as an author, you need to increase your sales rank. Maximizing your sales on only one platform will help you do that. The Kindle Select program easily allows you to create special promotions. Used in conjunction with other promotions, this can greatly increase your e-book sales. Think of it as the snowball effect: Increasing e-book sales in the specific weeks in which you run specials can increase your sales ranking. This gives you increased visibility on Amazon, which, in turn, increases your rankings.

To use the plan you must first make sure that your e-book is not available on any other platform except Kindle. If you have already uploaded your book to other sites, take it down. Then go to your Kindle Direct Publishing "bookshelf" and select the "Kindle Select" option, which increases your royalties to seventy percent.

Uploading Your Book

If your book is not yet listed anywhere, go straight to www.kdp.amazon.com. If you have not used the site before, you will be directed to the account setup section. As mentioned in earlier, to complete it you will need your Social Security number, bank routing number, and bank account number. You will be required to fill out a tax interview form. *Yes, you must do this because you want Amazon to pay you royalties.* To do so, Amazon must know where to send them, and you must pay taxes on them. You will not be allowed to upload books without completing this information.

Once you fill out your tax information, click on the "bookshelf" tab on the top left of the page. Click on "+ebook" square, and fill in the information.

Now you are ready to upload your manuscript. This may take anywhere from a few minutes to an hour depending on the size of the book, the number of links it has, and your Internet speed.

Once the book is uploaded, use the preview option to make sure it looks right. The program will also look for spelling mistakes. This is your last chance to make corrections. Look over the mistakes listed, make any corrections necessary, and upload again if needed. *If you plan to use the pre-order feature, make sure you have made all your corrections and re-uploaded before clicking "publish."* Once you have clicked "publish" with a pre-order, you will be able to make changes to your manuscript until seventy-two hours before your book goes on sale.

Upload your cover. If your cover does not follow the guidelines for number of pixels or other details, you must correct the problem and upload again. Next, check the "yes" button to enroll in KDP Select, making Amazon the sole distributor of your e-book.

Now select your price. I suggest $3.99 for the average first-time author with a fiction book or a general audience nonfiction book. You will then follow the form on the website, clicking on "all territories," the seventy percent royalty pricing, and if you also have a paper version of your book select Kindle Match, which allows a person who purchases a paper version of your book to also download the e-book. You can choose free or 99 cents for your Kindle Match. I also suggest you enable book lending (this is required if you are using KDP Select). Once you have done all these things, accept the terms and conditions. Now you are almost ready to publish.

Choose the date your book will be published. You can have your book available for sale immediately, or you can choose to have it listed as a pre-order for a few weeks or even months. I suggest using the pre-order option so that you can begin to create buzz about your book with your friends, family, fans, and social media contacts.

What Next?

Now that your book is on Amazon, tell people about it. For the first forty-five days of your e-book campaign, you will concentrate on asking the people you already know to buy and review your book. Your goal is to get ten reviews in this period.

After your first forty-five days on Amazon you can run a one-week price promotion, dropping your price either to 99 cents or free. For your first promotion, I suggest you go with 99 cents. You can then run an Amazon ad campaign, a Facebook ad campaign, or both.

In the Resources section of this book you will find a list of several e-book promotion sites. These sites put out daily newsletters to subscribers telling them about various books deals. The newsletter is free for subscribers but, as an author, you must pay to advertise. Prices run from about $25 to several hundred dollars, depending on the popularity of the site. Some sites increase the price for more popular genres such as mystery. These sites have had varying degrees of success. BookBub is the site that authors find most successful, but it is also the most difficult for your book to be accepted.

Once you have signed up for a date for your price promotion and set dates for your advertisements to run, make sure you go back to KDP and change your price for the dates you have selected. It's very easy to do.

On your bookshelf, look to the right of your book cover icon and click the "promote and advertise" icon. This will take you to a new page. Click on the yellow "Create a New Kindle Countdown Deal" button.

Create a new Kindle Countdown Deal

1. Select marketplace.

Kindle Countdown Deals are configured by marketplace. You can schedule one Kindle Countdown Deal in each available marketplace during your current KDP Select term.

Marketplace: Amazon.com

2. Choose when the promotion will start and end.

Kindle Countdown Deal promotions can run for up to 7 days.

Must be after July 31, 2017 (Why?)   Must be before October 24, 2017 (Why?)

Start: July 31, 2017   End:

8:00 AM PST   8:00 AM PST

3. Select the number of price increments for this promotion and the starting price. You will be able to view and edit your promotion schedule after clicking "Continue" below.

Number of price increments: 1   Starting list price $ 0.99   Ending list price $2.99 (original list price)
(What's this?)   (What's this?)

Make sure "Marketplace" is set to Amazon.com, not AmazonUK. Choose the date your deal will start and end. Then choose the price.

Now your first e-book promotion is set.

You cannot, however, just sit back and let it happen. Setting up your ad or using an e-book selling site will boost your sales, but you need to help it along. Post your deal on Facebook, Twitter, and other social media sites. If you have a newsletter, send one out the week of your sale and include a link to your book. Think about all the ways you can let people know that your book is on sale for a week at 99 cents.

Of course, there are no guarantees in life, and the first promotion will rarely take you to number one in your category, unless you happen to have a very small niche market. This does not mean that you should give up. A tiny percentage of books jump out of the gate at the number 1 ranking and make back the money spent on production in the first week or two. A more realistic goal is that over time you increase your sales, increase your rankings, and increase your fan base.

To continue to have sales, you must constantly find new readers. Unlike some products (staples such as food, shoes, or gasoline, for example), you will not get repeat customers for the same book. This means that you must continually look for new readers or watch your sales drop. Without marketing, you will not find new readers and your book's sales will fall slowly but surely in the rankings as other newer books grab readers' interest and sales.

As with all marketing, e-book promotions work best when done several times. You can run a promotion once a quarter. The objective, as I mentioned earlier, is to slowly, over time, watch your sales rank increase. It will be at its highest on the first day or two of a promotion but with luck, after each promotion your rank will stay higher for longer.

Reading Your Ranking

How do you know what your rank on Amazon is? It's actually very easy. Once your book is online, click on your product page and scroll down to the "Product details" section. I've printed the product details for a book on the next page.

First, you see various information about the book, including the file size, publisher, ASIN, the ISBN if it has one. At the bottom of the list you see "Amazon Best Sellers Rank." This gives you the overall rank, or how your book ranks in sales with all Kindle e-books in every category. Following are ranks in three categories. The rankings are updated daily, sometimes more than once a day, which is why keeping an eye on your rank throughout a sales promotion is important.

You can use this type of promotion whether you are with KDP Select or have chosen to publish your e-book on several sites. Each site has different rules about promotions, so make sure you read

---

Product details

File Size: 2240 KB
Print Length: 267 pages
Simultaneous Device Usage: Unlimited
Publisher: Can't Put It Down Books; 1 edition (October 16, 2015)
Publication Date: October 16, 2015
Sold by: Amazon Digital Services LLC
Language: English
ASIN: B016SI78IE
Text-to-Speech: Enabled ⌄
X-Ray: Not Enabled ⌄
Word Wise: Enabled
Lending: Enabled
Screen Reader: Supported ⌄
Enhanced Typesetting: Enabled ⌄
Amazon Best Sellers Rank: #182,575 Paid in Kindle Store (See Top 100 Paid in Kindle Store)
 #773 in Books > Science Fiction & Fantasy > Fantasy > **Magical Realism**
 #1206 in Kindle Store > Kindle eBooks > Science Fiction & Fantasy > Fantasy > **Fairy Tales**
 #1510 in Kindle Store > Kindle eBooks > Literature & Fiction > **Mythology & Folk Tales**

Would you like to **tell us about a lower price?**

---

everything very carefully before you start. You don't want to pay for a promotion and then find that you are not allowed to run it the week you have scheduled.

Rinse and Repeat

There is an old marketing story, I don't know if it is true or not, but it goes like this. An advertising executive was putting together a campaign for Prell shampoo. The company wanted to increase sales. The advertising executive suggested that the words "lather, rinse and repeat" be added to the label. Customers followed the instructions, began using twice as much shampoo during every shower, and the company increased sales.

What's the point? *You cannot do one e-book promotion and expect your book to become a best seller and stay at the top of the rankings. To increase sales you must "rinse and repeat."*

Set realistic goals for your book each time you plan an e-book marketing campaign. Just don't get disappointed if you don't make the number 1 rank on your first promotion. Continue to do e-book promotions quarterly. Mix it up a bit. Try different e-book promotion sites. Change the wording of your ads. Test the results of Amazon ads versus Facebook ads by running only one type of ad at a time. Use the list in the Resources section of this book to find sites to market your book, but also do some research on your own and discover other ideas. Different combinations of promotions seem to work best for different authors and different genres.

Don't just depend on one type of promotion. And when you are paying for advertising, bolster it by mentioning your promotion on Facebook, Twitter, TikTok, and any other social media sites you use. It takes time and work to gain recognition as an author, but it can be done.

Chapter 23
Using Social Media

Social networking is the third leg of the revolution that began with online bookstore sites and print-on-demand publishing. Together, these three things have changed publishing forever, taking it out of the hands of large, corporate publishing houses and placing it squarely in the hands of authors and independent publishers.

Social media allows us to connect with people around the world and personally tell them about our books. It allows the stereotypical, shy writer who is uncomfortable with the public spotlight to make connections and develop relationships without ever leaving the comfort of their home. It allows us to tell the world about our latest books without spending a lot of money. Of course, it can also be confusing and overwhelming to a beginning social networker.

When we think about social media marketing we often limit it to Facebook, Twitter, and LinkedIn, but it also includes blogging, YouTube, Meetup, Instagram, TikTok, Tumblr, Reddit, Kickstarter, and a host of other sites aimed at specific niche markets. As with all marketing, it takes time to do social networking well; as more and more sites spring up, it is not possible to be active on all of them. The best plan is to look at which sites are the favorites of your target readers, then pick only a few and really work at them consistently.

Which Sites Will Work for You?

A personal Facebook page is where you share about you, but you should also have a Facebook page for your book. If you are writing fiction or nonfiction for a general audience, Facebook is probably a site you want to concentrate on. However, it is not right for every author. If you have a professional or academic book, skip this site and spend your time on LinkedIn, a site that is more business related than Facebook.

Instagram and Pinterest are visual sites that use pictures and graphics. Both can be connected to your Facebook page. Pinterest is currently not as fashionable as Instagram but check out where your target readers are networking. If they are on Pinterest, you should be on Pinterest. If they are on Instagram, that's where you should be.

YouTube is an excellent place to post book trailers advertising your book as well as short, informative, or instructional videos that show your expertise in your subject and as a speaker.

Twitter is a way to draw attention to posts and videos on other sites. Its short messages make it perfect for a quick "teaser headline" directing people to a longer piece of information.

TikTok is also very popular with authors who are creating "Book Toks." TikTok uses very short videos, often filmed on a phone, so you don't need any special equipment to join in the fun.

There are many other sites out there; if you hear about one that interests you, get on and use it for a few days to see what type of things are posted. Think about how it can help you find your target market. If your readers are there, you should be, too.

Facebook Live

Facebook Live allows you to stream your own video. Before beginning to stream, it is best to announce it on Facebook a few hours, or even days, in advance so that interested people can be prepared to watch. However, once you have recorded it, it stays on your Facebook page and can be accessed and promoted again. My first try at Facebook Live was at our Winter Writers' Weekend, and I was impressed with the results. We streamed several workshops and had about fifty views for each at the time—that is fifty people who saw the workshop who were not able to attend in person. But the real success came over the next few weeks as we reposted the videos. Within the month each video had several hundred additional views.

Facebook Live is easy to do. You simply click on Facebook on your phone, then click on the "live" button. One tip we quickly learned: You must hold your phone sideways for the picture to show in the correct axis. Also, make sure your volume is on high and that you have a well-charged battery or a portable battery charger with you. That's all it takes for you to be live on Facebook!

Goodreads

Goodreads is a social networking site for book lovers. If you do only one thing on social media, it should be Goodreads. The first thing to do is to sign up as a reader. Get familiar with the site, fill out the information on what you are reading, join a few groups, and begin to participate in discussions.

As soon as your book is published and available online, sign into the author section and "claim" your book. Fill out some of the basic questions about your book, such as "what motivated you to write this book?" You can also sign up for a book giveaway if you have a paper book. You choose the number of books you will give away, post it on Goodreads, and people sign up for a chance to get a free book. Goodreads takes care of the details and sends you the names and addresses of the winners. I suggest you plan to give away five to ten books. You mail your book to the winners. Sign the books and add a nice note asking the winners to review your book.

While only a few people receive a free book, the giveaway can generate interest for you. During a recent giveaway by a young adult author I know, more than 800 people signed up. The final giveaway generated two reviews on Amazon and several book sales.

Kickstarter

Kickstarter is a site that helps people connect with the general public to crowdfund their projects. It is particularly targeted to the arts, publishing, film, and other creative projects. According to Kickstarter, the site is "where creators share new visions for creative work with the communities that will come together to fund them."

Kickstarter can work for new authors who are looking for money to fund the publication of a book as well as to build a fanbase for the author. Some authors have huge financial success with Kickstarter. But there is a caveat: If you don't raise all of the money you have asked for in the time you have allotted for the campaign, you get none of the money. It is refunded to those who pledged it.

Developing a Kickstarter project takes time, work, and the use of other social media to announce your campaign. Like most social media, this is not something that you just put online and expect it to create miracles for you. You must work at it.

If you are interested in using Kickstarter to fund a project and develop a fanbase, I suggest you first go to the site and look over some of the projects that are already listed and see how they work. Then look online for articles on how to use Kickstarter to help you with your book publishing goals.

Blogging

Many people forget about blogging when discussing social networking, but it's a very important part of the equation for an author. Blogging is, after all, an online journal, and many writers are avid journal writers. Because of this, a blog can become a place where writers experiment and spark their creativity by getting into the habit of writing on a daily basis.

Blogging, however, has one advantage over a private journal. Bloggers can also get feedback from their readers and promote their next books by posting book excerpts. They can write generally about their subject, repost articles and other bloggers' insights on their topic, become known in their field, and increase their search engine rankings.

Writing a blog is not that different from other types of writing. You want people to read your blog, just as you want them to find your book, buy it, and read it. Use Twitter to bring your followers to your blog. Not only should you be blogging on your own website but you should also consider guest blogging or blogging on a site such as shewrites.com or writing reviews on sites such as Goodreads. Find out which blogs and social networking sites your target readers frequent, and make sure you are also on those sites.

What Are Your Goals?

Until you decide on your specific goals for social networking, it is difficult to develop a strategy for which sites you should be on and what you should be posting. Your goals might include:

- Increase your professional contacts
- Become known as an expert

- Reconnect with old friends and colleagues
- Develop prospects for your business
- Demonstrate your abilities as a speaker
- Let people know about events
- Tell people about your book and where to buy it

These goals are very general, but they are a good starting point to help you come up with a more specific strategy. Sit down and think about what you would like a blog to do for you before you begin.

Consistency and Participation

No matter which sites you choose to use, if you aren't consistent in your posting, you won't get very far. My personal experience: I opened a Twitter account several years ago. I didn't really know why I was posting and, being a wordy writer, I had difficulty with the 280-character format. I would tweet once every few months or so, and for a couple of years my Twitter account languished with about fifty followers. Finally, I decided to really become consistent with my social networking. I got some help from an expert and really started to understand the why and how of Twitter. I began posting tweets several times a day. Guess what? My Twitter following began to increase daily. Within a few weeks I had more than 200 followers. Within a few months I had more than 2,000 followers, and now I'm close to 3,000 followers.

The secret to any social networking site is participation. If you don't check your sites regularly, it won't do you any good to be there. On LinkedIn, find discussion groups that relate to your book and participate in their discussions. Share tips and advice. Tweet daily and respond to tweets from your followers. The same is true of Pinterest, Facebook, and any other site you choose. Becoming a valued contributor increases your credibility and visibility and encourages book sales as well.

More About Blogging

If you are an author, you should be writing daily, which means you already have material ready and waiting to post on a blog. If you don't have a blog, set up a blog page on your website. If you don't have a website, set up a blog page. WordPress is one of the most popular sites to set up a blog. Go to wordpress.com, follow the steps, and set up your blog free in minutes. It really is that easy—and as you may have noticed as you read this book, I'm not a person who is particularly good with technology. So if I say it is easy, it *really is* easy.

Here are a few blogging tips to get you started.

- **Be consistent.** Blog at least once a week, then tweet about your blog and share it on Facebook and other social media.
- **Use keywords.** Think of several keywords people will use when searching for your topic, and use them in your blog posts.
- **Guest blog.** And return the favor. Research others who are blogging in related fields and ask them for guest posts.
- **Be patient.** It takes time to develop a following.

Social media is both the greatest thing to happen to entrepreneurs and small business owners—and as an author you are an entrepreneur—and the worst thing to happen. Social media has brought us the ability to connect with people all around the world and tell them about our products and our expertise. It can also be confusing, overwhelming, the fastest way to make a mistake, the quickest way to make an apology, and the easiest way to waste time while telling yourself you are actually being productive and "networking to promote your book."

There is always a "next big thing" in social media. There are a few sites currently gaining interest, or "trending" as they say in the social media world. TikTok went from being almost unknown to a becoming a household name in 2020. Other sites that are just gaining steam are Clubhouse and Twitter Spaces. They may or may not become the next big social media craze.

Text message marketing was a new thing when I wrote the first edition of this book. Unfortunately, it has become almost as ubiquitous as spam emails.

No matter which sites you use, or which new sites become popular in the future, social media is an excellent way to create interest in your book before it is finished. Share about the process of writing your book. Post paragraphs and excerpts. Ask for feedback. Use your social networking sites as a focus group. You can test out a title, versions of your cover, or ask for feedback on the development of a character if you are a fiction writer. Don't be shy. These are your followers. Let them know how excited you are about the publication of your book.

But talking just to friends is not enough to turn a book into a best seller. You also need to reach out to people you don't yet know. That is the secret to all marketing, and it is what makes social media an important tool for all authors to master.

Chapter 24
Build Your Brand

Branding is creating an image that comes immediately to mind when your name, the title of your book, your series of books, or your company name are mentioned. When the talk turns to brands a couple of companies with great brand strategy always come up, such as Nike and Coca-Cola. Talk about branding for books and what do you think of? Stephen King? Harry Potter? The *For Dummies* books? Ann Rice? Some of these are authors, and others are series titles; some are fiction, and some are nonfiction. But they are all brands with international recognition.

You, too, have a brand. It may not be internationally known, or even nationally known—yet. Among your friends, your clients, and your business colleagues you have a brand. Are you known as approachable or unapproachable? Reliable or unreliable? An expert people can turn to for advice or the last person to ask? You get the picture.

If you are already in business, you are developing this brand awareness for your business as well as for yourself. Now is the time to brand both your book for its excellent writing style and great information, and yourself as an expert author.

Branding is an enormous subject, and it has many aspects to it. If you discuss branding with a graphic artist, you will hear your business card, your website, and your book cover should all have one unified theme—the colors, fonts, overall tone, and style should match on every web page and every piece of paper you send out. If you talk to a business coach, you will hear about how to become a great referral partner. If you talk to a presentation coach, you will hear about style of dress and your elevator pitch. If you talk to someone in marketing, you will learn that you need a tagline, a great brand name, and interesting marketing copy. All these people are correct. Your brand involves all these things, and more.

Don't Outgrow Your Brand

Let's say you are a lifestyle coach starting out in business. You want to focus on helping people who need to lose weight so you choose a diet-related business name such as The Weight Loss Guru. After a few years you find this is too limiting. You want to talk to people who have health issues such as heart disease and diabetes and need to change the way they eat but are focusing on nutrition, rather than weight loss. Your brand, which you've spent a lot of time, money, and energy developing, no longer fits. You need to rebrand yourself. *It will be much easier and less expensive in the long run if you choose a brand that can grow right along with you.*

Branding is important for fiction authors as well as nonfiction authors. Nora Roberts, for example, was already famous for her romance novels when she decided to create her futuristic mystery series, which she writes under the pen name J.D. Robb. All the titles in her *In Death* series have the words "in death" in the title (for example, *Naked in Death* and *Brotherhood in Death*). The covers are also each stylistically the same. When you see the characteristic cover design and the name "J.D. Robb" or "in death" on the cover, you know you are getting a different type of book than one with the author name "Nora Roberts" on the cover.

What Constitutes Your Brand?

We'll start with the title. The title of your book cannot be boring or generic. It needs to be catchy, can be easily searched on the Internet, and one for which you can obtain a URL. Search your proposed title on the Internet and on Amazon. What do you come up with? Are there other similar sites and books? Or sites you don't want to be identified with? Just because there are similar titles or websites out there, you may not need to change your title. Check them out. They are your competition. How do you look in comparison to them?

However, if the name you choose puts you into a group of websites or books that have nothing to do with what you are writing about, you may want to rethink it.

When I was purchasing a website for my company, Open Door Publications, I thought it would be nice if the URL was short. "I'll make my URL 'OpenDoorPub,'" I said to myself. Well, you can imagine what came up when I tried a test search using that name. I was suddenly being placed with bars and taverns—not where I wanted my website to be. While my URL may be long, I find opendoorpublications.com helps people who are searching for publishing assistance locate me.

The best way to create a brand is to write more than one book on your subject. Think of a catchy, brandable, nongeneric name for your series. Most first-time authors don't start out with an idea for a series. Think ahead. If you do write a second book, what will it be called? How will it relate to your first book? The title, the font, and the style of the cover are all potential elements in branding your books and branding yourself.

I've mentioned this in several other areas but let me say it once again: If you do not have a website, get one. What is the most important thing you want people to remember? If you are writing one book and never plan to write another, the website URL should be the title of the book. Do you want to use your book as a springboard for a speaking or consulting career? Your URL should be your name. Do you have a business associated with your book? Use that name as your website. Or consider all three choices. It is not really possible to buy every URL associated with you, your book, or your business, but do consider owning several. Owning several URLs does not mean that you must develop several websites. They can all link back to one website.

Brand Yourself

Whether you are writing fiction or nonfiction, you are the brand. Your bio should reflect that. We tend to err in one of two ways on our biographies: either we are too modest and embarrassed to talk about our true accomplishments, or we get too full of ourselves and throw around adjectives and phrases such as "world-class," "new and innovative approach," or "unique." These words and phrases are ultimately meaningless. Your bio should talk about you and your accomplishments in an interesting way that makes the reader want to learn more about what you have to say; in other words, it needs to be about what makes the reader want to buy your book.

You may think you are the best person to write your bio because you know yourself best, but that is often the problem—you know yourself too well. Once you have written your bio, let several people read it. See what they think you forgot to mention, or what you mention that is unimportant. Better still, get a professional writer to write your bio for you.

Social media can also help you create your brand. Don't simply make connections and friends on various social media sites; get to know the people. Write blog articles about your subject and post them on a variety of websites. Join groups on LinkedIn and actively participate. Offer advice and help to others. Make sure you are known not just as an expert but as someone who is willing to share your knowledge and help others.

Another way to spread the word about you and your brand is to work with the media. The first step: When the media call, answer. I was a news reporter for more than twenty years, and one thing never changed: A source who answers the phone or returns calls promptly will be used again and again. The reverse is also true: The source who is difficult to get in touch with, who is reluctant to answer questions, or who does not return calls in a timely fashion won't be on a reporter's short list when an expert is needed. What does this have to do with branding? Getting your name out there as an expert improves your brand.

Some people have the idea that if they share their knowledge with others, it will make that knowledge less valuable, or it will in some way be used against them. This is something I've seen many times in calling sources for news stories and features.

Some people I call love to help. They want to share with others, particularly someone just starting out. They know by helping others they will help themselves. Others are afraid to talk to me. They think if someone else learns their "secrets of success," they themselves will have less success. Sharing your knowledge not only helps to increase others' awareness of your expertise but it brands you as a person who cares enough to share with others.

Finally, be approachable. An author I know recently attended a convention where a number of other better-known authors were holding seminars and book signings. He attended several and stood in line at each to have a book autographed. Two authors, both well-known inspirational writers, had very distinct but different styles at their book signings. One quickly wrote her name in each book without looking up or speaking to the fans who had just purchased her book. The second author, who had just as many people lined up at her table, spent a few moments talking to each person who approached her and personalized each signature she wrote.

Both authors left definite impressions on my friend. But which author's books do you think he will continue to seek out and purchase and which do you think he will ignore? People will often buy books based upon their perceptions of the author—not only their knowledge, writing style, storytelling ability, or expertise but their personality as well. Make sure your brand is that of a friendly, helpful, approachable person. It will help you sell more books.

You might not be signing books at conventions yet, but you are out there in the author world, creating an impression. One of the easiest ways to help other authors is to review their books on Amazon, Goodreads, and other appropriate websites. Giving reviews is helping yourself while helping others. Spending a few minutes to post a good review about someone else's book will only bring good things to you. It increases your searchability on the web, it increases your reputation as an expert, and since you will list your book and your URL in your signature, it will bring you more book sales and drive traffic to your website. But more than any of these things, you will be acting as a friend.

If you read a book and you enjoy it, you will probably pick up the next book that author writes. That's what branding as an author is all about. We trust the author will continue to supply us with high quality with interesting and informative material. Quality counts. You want your brand to stand for quality and professionalism in everything you do.

Chapter 25
Marketing Fiction

Most of the publishing experts I have spoken with agree fiction is more difficult to market than nonfiction. There is so much more of it out there. There are so many genres and sub-genres and sub-sub-genres. Also, readers' opinions about fiction are much more subjective. What one reader loves, the next hates, and there is no right or wrong. It's all about what the reader likes. Here are some tips particularly for fiction writers. This does not mean there aren't great tips that apply to fiction in the rest of this book—there are but these tips are especially for you.

Let me repeat this one more time: ***The day you quit marketing your book is the day it stops selling.*** It is just as important to market fiction as it is nonfiction, yet I've often found that it is the fiction writer who is the most reluctant to put themself out there, whether from modesty or shyness, or a sense that artists shouldn't be bothered with mundane things like selling their work. Talk to any successful writer in any genre, and you will learn a large part of being an author is not about writing at all; it is about Authorpreneurship. That means getting out there and meeting people, setting up book readings and lectures and interviews, and learning about the business of selling your books. If you want to have the time and money to write, you have to take the time to market. Here are some specific marketing strategies that work.

Get a Booth

Get a booth at a book festival, and get yourself in front of readers. There are book festivals in every state. They range from gigantic, several day affairs, such as the Miami Book Fair

International or the Virginia Festival of the Book or the Romance Writers' of America, to smaller events such as the Collingswood, Book Festival in New Jersey. Many libraries and local bookstores also hold smaller events for local authors. The best resource I know to learn about book festivals in the United States is at www.bookfestival.com. It lists book festivals throughout the country. You can surely find one near you. Check the festival out online and see what the organizers say about it. Is this the right festival for you? What do you need to bring? If it is outdoors, do you need to bring your own tent, or will one be supplied for you? These are just a few of the questions you should think about when signing up to display your books at a festival. Don't forget events such as Comic-Cons if you write fantasy or science fiction. Town festivals are also a good place for local authors to sell their books. Be creative and think about all the different types of festivals that might work for your book.

Festivals and other events are wonderful, but you still must balance the time you spend with this type of selling versus promoting your book on Amazon.

The pros of event selling are:

- You keep a larger share of the profit versus a royalty from Amazon.
- You get to meet and interact with your readers. It's a good way to develop loyal fans.
- You get to network with other authors and learn from them.

The cons of event selling are:

- You must weigh the cost of the booth with the potential for sales. The higher the booth price, the more books you need to sell to break even.
- Don't forget to add in the cost of gas, lunch, and possibly an overnight stay at a hotel.
- It takes time to drive to the location and a lot of energy to lug boxes of books and other items to your booth, then take them down and pack them in your car at the end of the event.
- If the event is outdoors, bad weather can ruin not only your day but your product as well. You can't sell books that have gotten wet.

- The sales you make at events will never increase your best seller ranking.

Enter a Contest

There are hundreds of contests out there: large and small, regional and national, genre-specific and general. There are contests for self-published authors and contests for unpublished authors. Find one and enter it. If you win, it can really boost your writing career. If you don't, some contests do offer feedback from the judges. If all else fails, you've lost nothing more than your entry fee.

"What!" I hear you shouting in protest. "I have to spend money to enter a contest? What if I don't win? That's money wasted."

Yes, you do have to spend money, either on contests or on something else. I've seen the notes on various LinkedIn groups, and I've heard the complaints from writers I know. Yes, you have to spend money even if you don't know if you will earn it back. And yes, those entry fees can start to add up over the course of a year. You are in business. You cannot be in business without spending some money. For the fiction writer, entering contests is an excellent marketing tool and a legitimate marketing expense.

Reviews

While we talked a lot about reviews in previous chapters, it is worth mentioning again here because reviews are one of the most important strategies for fiction writers. As I mentioned in the opening paragraph of this chapter, readers' feelings about the fiction they read are highly subjective and extremely personal, so a great review on the right website can really boost your book sales.

Create Interest for Your Book Online

If you don't have a website, start one today. Share your writing in a blog, on Internet groups—there are dozens out there—and in local writing groups. Use meetup.com to find groups in your area.

LinkedIn and Yahoo are other good ways to connect with writers. Many writers have developed a following for their work by using these groups to generate interest in their characters and story before their book is published. Since the pandemic, even more groups have gone online, making it even easier for you to find them, contact them, and suggest that you would make a great speaker for their group. With Zoom and other online services, you can easily be the speaker at a book group anywhere in the world. And if you have ever been in a book group, you know that the chance for members to talk with the author of the book they are reading is almost always accepted.

Work With Schools

Many schools bring writers in for workshops, writer-in-residence programs (even elementary schools), and readings. Sometimes the writer is paid; other schools don't have the money. There are also arts grants and state and regional programs financed by either the government or an arts council that will bring writers into schools. Search the Internet for programs in your area.

Depending on the situation (whether you are talking with parents or students), you may or may not be allowed to actually sell your book directly at the school. If the school is not paying you to speak, you may be able to arrange for them to purchase enough copies of the book for each of the students that you speak with, or a few copies for the school library. If you are talking about classroom sets, schools do expect to give a discount. School budgets are always tight but working with a school still has many advantages: You can develop a relationship and be asked to return year after year, and you can often get some newspaper coverage for yourself and the school (make sure you check with the school before you contact the newspaper). Finally, you are giving something to the students and your community, and you have the opportunity to help young people gain an appreciation and knowledge of literature and your subject.

Give a Reading

Giving readings is one of the most important ways that fiction authors can market their work. It is the most tangible sample of your work that you can give to your readers. When you give a reading, not only do you have the opportunity to read your work but you can also answer questions about how you developed your plot and your characters, giving additional information that will make the reader more interested not only in buying the book you are reading from but your other work—written or not yet written—as well. You can set up your own book tour by contacting libraries, arts organizations, or other groups that will be interested in your subject. For instance, historical fiction writers should contact history groups or museums. There are also cafes and coffee shops that hold open mic nights and poetry readings. Put your thinking cap on, and you can probably come up with a dozen or more locations you can do readings at within a few hours of your home.

Write Another Book

For fiction writers this is even more important than for nonfiction writers. If you are writing children's books, it is essential. Everyone loves to read a book by an author they already know. They have a sense of familiarity; they know what they are going to get. If you have created compelling characters, your readers want to know more about them. Once you get readers involved in the first book, it is much easier to get them to buy the second…and the third…and…

When promoting your second book, always mention the first book. Bring all your books with you to your readings, and consider some type of "twofer" promotion to encourage your listeners to buy more than one of your books.

Develop Add-On Products

Games, toys, CDs, t-shirts, mousepads, iPad cases…the list is endless. If you're a fiction writer, you've got a great imagination. What add-on products can be offered with your book? It's easy if you are a children's writer. Toys or dolls are a natural. Computer games are obvious for the fantasy writer. Add-ons can work for any genre; just use your imagination.

Brand Yourself and Your Books

Several of the tips in this chapter involve branding, which we talked about in Chapter 24. Branding is all about making your name and the names of your books familiar to the public. It can be as simple as making sure the covers of your books have a similar look and feel—particularly important if you are writing a book series.

Chapter 26
Workshops, Seminars, Other Events

Events are one of the best ways to market both yourself and your book. Every author should learn to be comfortable speaking in front of an audience. When you speak to people, you connect on a deeper level; now they feel as if they know you. Not only does that make them more likely to buy your book and read it but they are likely to recommend it to their friends, too.

But how do you get invited to speak before a group? Don't sit around waiting to get invited—ask! Let people know you would love to speak in front of their group. I've been on the programming committee of more than one organization and, believe me, most groups are always looking for speakers. It would be great to start your speaking career with a paid engagement at a national meeting, but most speakers don't start off that way. Speaking to smaller audiences is often free, but most organizations will allow you to bring your book and sell it at the back of the room, giving you the opportunity to make a free engagement pay for itself.

There are other benefits to speaking at an event. As the guest speaker you have instant credibility as an expert, and that can translate into more and better speaking gigs, client referrals, and media interviews.

If you can't find someone to host you, host your own event. There are several advantages to putting together your own event. You can choose the time and place and set things up in the way you are most comfortable, and you can set your own fees. Your event can be as simple or as elaborate as you would like to make it. You can even invite other guest speakers and create a full-day or weekend program.

Of course, when there is a positive, there is also a negative. When you create your own event, you are in charge of everything—finding the event site, inviting the speakers, publicizing the event, collecting the fee, and paying the bills. You can always delegate some of these tasks to other people, but in the end the responsibility is yours. An event can cost you from next to nothing for a simple lunch in which everyone pays for their own meal to literally thousands of dollars for a weekend seminar. Start small. Learn how to host a small event before you graduate to something larger and costlier.

There are so many aspects to hosting an event it would take an entire book to discuss them all. Since this is a book on selling your book, we will stick to the marketing aspect of event planning. Even if you are an invited guest speaker, you can help the organizers promote the event. The more people who attend, the better. You will become known as a speaker who can bring in an audience, putting you more in demand.

I have noticed at events I have organized and events I have spoken that very few of the other speakers promote the event. They are doing themselves and the organization a great disservice. If you are invited to speak somewhere, tell others about it. Tell your clients. Tell your friends. Tell your fans. Use your newsletter. Use social media. And while you are telling people about the event make sure that you mention how they can register for it. Helping to make the event a success means that you will be asked back again and again. Do blow your own horn. If you know that you are responsible for certain guests at an event, tell the hosts just how many people came specifically because of you.

Promote Yourself to Organizations

Create a list of organizations you would like to speak for.

Start local: What groups do you belong to? Who do you know who belongs to a group you would like to get in front of?

Move to regional: Once you've spoken in front of a local chapter, ask the program chairman or president for referrals to other chapters in the state or region. Think about state conventions. They always need workshop and seminar presenters, as well as keynote speakers. Find out who is organizing these events and contact them.

Go national: There are hundreds of conventions every year. At which ones would you like to be a guest speaker or presenter? Add them to your list and send out a press kit. A few hours of online research should garner some good leads. Start by Googling organizations you know. Also, try some more generic searches such as "animal charities" or "women's organizations."

No one wants to buy a pig in a poke. If you are selling your speaking abilities, you need to give out a sample. A three- to five-minute video is all you need. If you have a speaking engagement already booked, ask if you can videotape it. If you are speaking at an online event, the organizers may be taping. Ask for a copy of the file. If you are speaking at an in-person event, consider bringing your own videographer—someone who knows how to create a great video and can be discreet while doing it. You don't want your videographer getting in the way of someone else's meeting. It's just not polite.

If you don't have a speaking engagement coming up soon, fake it. The beauty of video is that your audience sees just what you want them to see. Dress up, stand in front of a neutral background, and have yourself videotaped making a speech. You can use Zoom to create your own video, or have a someone tape you. Have the person doing the taping zoom in on you; no one will know a crowd of a hundred isn't sitting in front of you.

Develop a separate press kit to send out to organizations where you would like to speak. Along with everything in your regular press kit, your speaker's kit should include a separate page listing speaking engagements you have already made as well as speech and seminar topics you can cover. Include a copy of your book as well. One of the most important things for you to include is a link to a video of yourself speaking on your topic so that the organizers can see you in action.

Tell Everyone

Once you have an engagement booked, tell everyone about it. Yes, pat yourself on the back. This isn't bragging. As I mentioned earlier, as a guest speaker, one of your goals should be to help the organization bring as many people to the event as possible. Post the event on Facebook. Tweet about it. Mention it on LinkedIn. Add it to the events section of your website. Mention it in your monthly newsletter. Letting the world know you are available as a speaker will bring more invitations.

Ask the organizer about other media opportunities surrounding the event. Local organizations may have their meetings featured in the local newspaper. Larger events may get local television media coverage. Make yourself available for any publicity opportunities.

Online Events

Even before the pandemic, online events were becoming popular. The events of 2020 just hastened things along. Even people who disliked using computers and scorned the thought of being able to make connections online found themselves relying on Zoom, Skype, and other apps to maintain connections with friends, family, co-workers, and others.

And suddenly we realized there were some advantages to meeting online.

That conference we couldn't afford to go to because the airfare and hotel reservations were just too expensive was suddenly available to us while sitting in our PJs. The networking group we usually missed because it was just too early in the morning became not only feasible but a welcome way to connect with other humans.

For authors, there has been both an upside and a downside to the increase in online events. The upside: We can easily give book talks to groups all over the world. We can make connections with more people and let them know about our books. Book groups have welcomed having authors chat with them via Zoom.

The downside: It's more difficult to sell books at the back of the room when meeting virtually with someone. Publishing a link to your Amazon page is just not as effective as standing at a table with books ready to autograph for them. The best strategy to get around this problem is to work with the organizer to purchase a certain number of books ahead of the event and have them sent directly to the attendees. It won't work every time or for every event, but it is one sure way to make sure your book talks turn into sales.

Sell Your Books

When setting up the speaking engagement, make sure you ask the organizer if you can bring your books to sell. Most organizations will not have a problem with this, but sometimes the event just isn't suitable for this type of selling. Churches and synagogues, for example, may be sensitive about where and how a product is sold. Schools will not let you sell directly to children. Confirm with the event organizer that you have permission to sell your books, and get it in writing if you have a contract.

Some groups will allow you to set up a table at the back of the room. If it is a large group, they may supply a person to handle the book sales or they may ask you to bring someone to deal with it. If it is a small group of twenty people or less, you can probably handle the sales transactions yourself.

Some organizations may want a cut of the sales. It's only fair; they are, after all, supplying you with a captive audience to listen to your sales pitch. It is your choice whether or not to make this type of arrangement. Just be clear on percentages, recordkeeping, and other details before you arrive at the event.

Bring bookmarks, flyers, business cards, and other promotional materials to hand out during your talk. Make sure your website, book title, ISBN, and other contact information appear prominently on all this material—and also make sure it looks professional. Nothing will detract from a great talk and a great-looking book more than a sloppy handout.

Ask the organizers if you may have a list of the people who attended your speech, preferably with emails. Be sure to get permission to use the email addresses so people are not surprised by emails they may consider as spam. And make sure that you add an unsubscribe option to your emails.

Another way to collect contact information is to raffle one of your books as a door prize. Ask the organizers first. Most will be thrilled to let you give away something to their members. Collect business cards in a basket and raffle the book at the end of your speech or at the end of the meeting. At most business meetings it is assumed the person who is donating the prize will use these cards to add to their contact list. But again, make sure that your audience understands this and won't be offended by a follow-up email.

Chapter 27
Keep the Sales Going

There was a time, not too long ago, when books were seen as something ephemeral. Traditional book publishers put out a book, heavily promoted it for three to six months, and then moved on to the next book, leaving the first one to languish on bookstore sales tables and remainder bins.

Authors, of course, have never liked this method of marketing, and as authors and small, independent publishing houses have become more prominent, they have come up with a different technique. It's called "wag the long tail." This phrase means you want to find ways to keep selling your book for several years—not just several months.

So how do you do this? You keep right on marketing. Remember Marketing Rule Number 2? The day you quit marketing your book is the day it quits selling. Well, the corollary is also true: As long as you continue to market your book, it will continue to sell.

Salespeople know it as "ABC"—always be closing. Remind people that you and your book are still out there. Keep up the social networking, continue to write your blog, and book more seminars and public speaking engagements.

When your book first comes out, no one has yet read it so it may be easier to rack up sales in the first few months. Once the majority of your tribe has bought your book, you can't expect sales to maintain the same pace. Unlike commodities such as food and clothing, once we have purchased one copy of a book (maybe two if we give one as a gift), we never need to purchase that book again.

This does not, however, mean you should stop promoting your book just because you have maxed out sales to your family, friends and fans. There are always new people moving into your sphere of influence—people you have not met before or people who have just become interested in the subject you are writing about. You may not sell hundreds books a month, but ten or fifteen sales a month will add to your bottom line. The trick is to maintain visibility even when you don't have a new book on the market. After all, it takes time to produce a book. You can't put a new one out each month.

Brick-and-mortar bookstores don't have the space for the slow-but-steady seller. To make money they need to specialize in hot, new titles. Online stores, however, have unlimited shelf space. Make sure your book is available on Amazon and other book selling websites, but think about other types of stores, too.

Is there an online specialty store catering to your target market? If your book is about a particular sport, particularly a smaller sport such as lacrosse or rowing, there are online retailers devoted specifically to them. Crafters and hobbyists of all kinds have their own websites. Fiction writers can benefit from this technique, too. There are websites devoted to romance, mystery, and science fiction, as well as other genres. Do the research, approach the site's owners, and see if you can sell your book, post a blog article, or purchase an advertisement.

Watch the News

Is there a breaking news event that ties in with your subject matter? Don't hesitate. Put out a press release immediately, and call attention to the fact that: (1) you are an expert in the field, and (2) you have written a book on the subject. HARO (helpareporterout.com) is an excellent way to keep on top of breaking news as well as to identify journalists who are working on stories about your topic. Sign up to get regular emails from this site, which specializes in connecting reporters with experts.

Calendar tie-ins can also generate news. What annual events can be used to promote your book? If your book is aimed at women, it would make a great Mother's Day gift. A book about planning a wedding should have a special promotion every June. Ghost stories sell in October, and anything about Irish heritage does well around St. Patrick's Day.

What calendar events can you use to promote your book? Don't just think of the big days, such as Christmas or Valentine's Day.

There are hundreds of special days, from the well-known such as Arbor Day to National Grammar Day (bet you didn't know about that one), that you can capitalize on. Don't forget special weeks and months such as Women's History Month and African American History month, too. Find yours and promote your book.

Seminars and Events

Do you give speeches or hold seminars and workshops—online or in person? Make sure you always have your book available to sell at any event where you are speaking. The audience is obviously interested in what you have to say so make sure they have the opportunity to take your book home with them.

Use your book as a giveaway to add value to a seminar, workshop, or other promotion. "If you sign up for my seminar now, you'll receive my book as part of the package." It's a tried-and-true marketing technique—and it works.

This also works for e-books. You can offer the e-book as part of that "sign up for my event" promotion, or once you have two books available, do a free promotion on your first book, particularly if it is part of series. You are only giving your book away for one week, and readers will get hooked on book one and immediately purchase book two. I speak from experience here—not as an author but as a reader. I will often use a free e-book promotion to try out a new author. There are many times I'm so hooked that immediately on finishing the first book, I go to Amazon and purchase the second.

Two-for-One and Other Offers

What other products do you sell? Promote your book in conjunction with one of your other products. For example, Book A sells alone for $15. Book B sells alone for $10. If purchased separately, your customer will have spent $25. Sell the books together for $20. Everyone wants a bargain. You'll be amazed at how many people will buy the two together. Think of the packages you see at most bookstores. You don't have to have a special box to make a two-for-one offer. An audio tape or CD and a toy that ties in with a children's book are all excellent choices for a two-for-one offer. Again, this approach also works for e-book series. Book one, the older book, sells for $2.99. Book two, the newer book, sells for $3.99. Create a combined e-book version that sells for $5.99. The price combinations can change and increase as you add more books to your series.

Write Another Book

I mentioned this in the Chapter 25 on marketing fiction, but it goes for writers of all genres. The best way to continue selling your first book is to write a second one. Make sure when you promote your second book that you always mention your first book. Bring both books with you to those seminars and speaking events, and mention the first book in press releases and during interviews. Writing a second book makes your first book fresh.

Chapter 28
From Writer to Author

At least once a week I meet someone new, and when I tell this person what I do the reply is: "I've got this great idea I've always wanted to turn into a book—if I could only find the time."

Yes, everyone wants to be an author, but no one really wants to be a writer. What's the difference? An author is a person who has completed and published something. A writer is a person in the middle of that process.

How do you move from writer to author? Sit down and start to write. It sounds so simple, but this is the step when most people fail: They never find the time to sit down and write so their book remains in their heads where it does no good for anyone, not even themselves.

It can be overwhelming to start a project as large as a book, even if it is a small book. To borrow a well-known proverb: How do you eat an elephant? One bite at a time. How do you write a book? One step at a time. I hope this book helps you divide your elephant into bite-sized pieces so that the task doesn't seem quite so overwhelming.

It is so much easier to say, "Just write it," than it is to actually sit down and write. But the bottom line is, if you want to be an author, you have to first sit down and be a writer. Don't wait for the perfect moment to happen before you start to write your book; that day when all your chores are done, your children are napping, your mother hasn't called, and your dog has been walked. That day will never happen. Instead, you have to work to schedule the time, find the energy, and look for the inspiration. Remember, to become an author you must first be a writer.

How do you measure success? Is it the number of books you

have sold? Receiving a great review of your book by a writer you admire? Being asked to give a speech about the subject of your book? Being able to put "author" on your bio? Having people tell you they were inspired by your book? Maybe it's all these things.

In today's digital world it is much easier than ever to publish a book. But as I've pointed out throughout this book, if you want someone to read it, you must tell people it is out there, and that means marketing.

I've been working with people in writing and other creative fields for over twenty-five years, and one of the common threads I've noticed is many writers are reluctant to market their work. Let me admit right here that I used to be one of these people. When I finally got over my fears and put myself out there, I was amazed at how quickly things changed for me. I sold more books, had more calls to write as a freelancer and, most surprisingly of all to me, groups and organizations started asking me to speak at their meetings.

I hope this book has inspired you to go out and write your book, publish it, and then market it. Don't put it off any longer. Start today.

Resources

There are many resources available for writers, both in print and on the Internet. It's not too surprising, I suppose, that writers love to write about writing. Here are some of my favorite resources.

The Craft of Writing

How to Write a Damn Good Novel and *How to Write a Damn Good Novel II*, James N. Frey, published by St. Martin's Press. The best books I've read on the craft of writing fiction. If you'd like to be a better fiction writer, I recommend these books. Nonfiction writers can learn a few things from them, too.

On Writing Well, William Zinsser, published by HarperCollins. An excellent book on the craft of writing.

Inventing the Truth: The Art and Craft of Memoir, William Zinsser, published by Houghton Mifflin Harcourt. Memoir is its own animal, a blend of fiction and nonfiction. If you want to write a memoir, check out this book.

Finish Your Book! A Time Management Guide for Writers, Karen Hodges Miller and Lorette Pruden, published by Open Door Publications. The second book in my own Write Your Book! series. It offers a number of useful tips on finding the time, the place, and the creative energy needed to finish the book you have always wanted to write.

On Writing by Stephen King, published by Scribner. Whether or not you are a fan of Stephen King's books, *On Writing* is considered by many as one of the best books on the craft of writing.

Style Guides

The Chicago Manual of Style, University of Chicago Press. The final say for all issues of style in book writing.

The Associated Press Stylebook, Basic Books. The essential style guide for newspaper and magazine writers.

Publication Manual of the American Psychological Association, American Psychological Association. The most common guide for the social sciences. Use for academic writing.

AMA Manual of Style, Oxford University Press. An online version is also available at www.amamanualofstyle.com.

The ACS Style Guide: Effective Communication of Scientific Information, American Chemical Society. The guide for science writers.

Finding an Agent

There are dozens of websites with listings for agents. Two that I am most familiar with are:

Poets & Writers: www.pw.org/magazine. This magazine offers excellent information for writers, including a listing of agents in its Tools for Writers section.

Writers' Market: www.writersmarket.com. A resource for writers on a wide variety of topics, and also offers a listing of agents.

Book Proposals

If you plan to look for an agent, you need a book proposal. Here are two excellent resources for nonfiction writers:

Bestselling Book Proposals: The Insider's Guide to Selling Your Work by Rick Frishman and Robyn Freedman Spizman, published by Adam's Media.

How to Write a Book Proposal by Michael Larsen, published by Writer's Digest Books.

Marketing Your Work

Writer's Market. This is the bible for writers and authors. It includes listings for magazines, book publishers, and agents, as well as tips on selling your work. Not only is there a yearly hardcover edition of the main *Writer's Market*, but there are also special editions for children's writers, poets, novel and short story writers, as well as others.

How to Make Real Money Selling Books (Without Worrying About Returns): A Complete Guide to the Book Publishers' World of Special Sales by Brian Jud. Jud is president of Book Marketing Works, a consulting firm established to help independent publishers market their titles to non-bookstore outlets. He is host of the television series *The Book Authority* and is a regular speaker on marketing topics at Independent Book Publishers Association's (IBPA's) Publishing University.

Dan Poynter's Self-Publishing Manual: How to Write, Print and Sell Your Own Book by Dan Poynter, Para Publishing. A nationally known expert, Poynter has over a dozen books on writing, publishing, and marketing books.

ADVANTAGE: Harnessing Cumulative Advantage in the Winner Takes All Publishing Market by Joe Solari explains the marketing theory of cumulative advantage and how you can use it specifically to increase your sales on Amazon.

Online Resources

When you're in the middle of writing, you don't want to be interrupted, even by something as simple as checking a spelling or looking up a definition. That's when the Internet really helps. Here are some great online resources that make writing just a little easier:

www.dictionary.com. There are lots of dictionary sites out there, but I find this one of the easiest to use for a quick spelling or definition check.

www.thesaurus.com. Don't depend on the little thesaurus feature you'll find in Microsoft Word. As part of the dictionary.com site, this website makes Roget's complex book obsolete.

www.brainyquote.com. This is a feature of Google and one of my favorites. If you need a quote on almost any subject under the sun, you can find it here.

www.grammerly.com. A great, free resource you can add to your software to correct mistakes on the fly. I use it all the time for emails and business writing. It might be a little annoying, however, for novel writers who may have characters who do not always use the best grammar when they speak. Try it out and see if you like it.

Book Review Sites

There are a number of websites devoted to book reviews. They include both general review sites and sites devoted to specific genres.

www.goodreads.com. One of the largest online resources for readers. Its users recommend books, compare what they are reading, keep track of what they've read and would like to read, find their next favorite book, form book clubs, and more. It offers a program for authors to promote their books.

LibraryThing is another member-based review site at http://www.librarything.com/

The Book Trap offers resources for readers at http://thebooktrap.weebly.com/readers-resource/the-midlist

The Indie View offers a very large list of book reviewers at http://www.theindieview.com/indie-reviewers/

Copyright

The U.S. Copyright Office can be found at www.copyright.gov. You'll find a lot of useful information on copyright law. You can also register your book online or file a claim.

E-Commerce

www.payloadz.com. PayLoadz offers a secure Digital Goods e-commerce service to sell downloadable goods such as e-books.

www.e-junkie.com. This shopping cart service can be used for both digital and tangible goods.

www.paypal.com. Both Payloadsz and E-junkie work well with PayPal, a site that allows you to take credit cards online and invoice customers.

E-Book Resources

Kindle Direct Publishing at https://kdp.amazon.com/en_US/ Everything you need to know about publishing an e-book for Amazon Kindle can be found on this site.

https://press.barnesandnoble.com is Barnes & Nobles' site for publishing books for the Nook e-reader.

www.smashwords.com. Read the "How to Publish on Smashwords" section thoroughly before you begin.

www.kobo.com/writinglife. Along with allowing you to upload your book, the Kobo site also offers interesting information.

Websites

Wordpress.com. A good site to host your blog or website.

GoDaddy.com. Purchase your URL, webhosting, and other

services.

theauthorwebsite.com. An excellent place for the do-it-yourself to get a good looking, inexpensive website. The template-based site allows authors to choose from a variety of designs and put up a website within a few minutes.

Silverhoopedge.com. Lisa Snyder of Silver Hoop Edge is my website designer, and I can't say enough good things about her. If you want a custom website, this is the place to go.

Amazon Resources

Maximize your listing at Amazon Author Central.
For information on Amazon reviewers, go to Amazon's Top Reviewers list at http://www.amazon.com/review/top-reviewers

Other Resources

Bowker Book Services
To obtain an ISBN and barcode and learn about other publishing services, go to www.bowker.com

Keyword Search Sites

If you are having trouble thinking of keywords to use for your website, there are a number of free keyword generator sites available online.

www.SEOBook.com: Go to the tools section of this site for the generator.

Grants for Writers

Poets and Writers, a magazine website with a lot more information than just grants, at www.pw.org

Mid-Atlantic Arts Foundation at www.midatlanticarts.org, for writers in the mid-Atlantic states. There are similar organizations in different regions of the country and many states.

Funds for Writers is a good website with a wealth of interesting information at www.fundsforwriters.com

Reposting Sites

The best way to gain more credibility from your blog posts is to repost them to other sites. Here are three popular sites. There are dozens of others.

www.digg.com
www.shewrites.com
www.reddit.com

E-Book Promotions

These sites send out daily newsletters to readers detailing e-book promotions. Costs vary. I recommend you sign up for a site and use it for a few weeks to understand how it works before you use it for a promotion. Most of the sites listed here require you to have **ten customer reviews on Amazon.**

www.Bookbub.com has one of the largest subscriptions, costs the most, and is the hardest on which to be accepted, but if you do get a promotion on it, you will make back your money.

www.Ereadernewstoday.com A favorite of mine for romance, general fiction, and nonfiction.

Some other sites that authors I know have used successfully are:
www.bargainbooksy.com
www.robinreads.com
www.thefussylibrarian.com

There are many other sites out there that offer similar services. Don't just stop at this list; go online and research more. Experiment and find out which work the best for you. It is all about finding out which sites your potential readers are using.

Acknowledgments

If there is one thing that I hope I have made obvious in the last twenty-eight chapters, it is that it takes a village to make a book.

Here is a special thanks to everyone in my own little village: Vivian Fransen, proofreader and Queen of the Comma; Noelle Stary, marketing expert and all-around good friend; Lisa Snyder, website specialist; and Eric Labacz, great graphic artist.

And, of course, special thanks to Sam, who always puts up with me when I'm in the middle of writing a book.

About the Author

Karen Hodges Miller is CEO at Open Door Publications, a company that specializes in helping authors navigate the world of publishing in the twenty-first century. The company assists both published and first-time authors with the wide variety of skills and tasks needed to successfully write, publish, and market a book.

Karen herself has written eight books, both fiction and nonfiction, as well as countless newspaper and magazine articles in her thirty-plus-year career. *How to Sell Your Book Today*, is her latest publication on book marketing techniques. The second edition of *Self-Publishing: You Can Do This!* is her most recent book, published in early 2022. A second book to be published in 2022, tentatively titled *Authorpreneurship*, focuses on authors as small business owners and the skills they need to be successful.

You can find out more about Karen Hodges Miller at www.opendoorpublications.com and KarenHodgesMiller.com, as well as on Facebook (www.facebook.com/OpenDoorPublications), on Twitter @Publisher_KHM, and on LinkedIn.

www.ingramcontent.com/pod-product-compliance
Lightning Source LLC
Chambersburg PA
CBHW060827050426
42453CB00008B/610